EARN COLLEGE CREDIT

FOR

WHAT YOU KNOW

Third Edition

EARN COLLEGE CREDIT

FOR

WHAT YOU KNOW

Third Edition

Lois Lamdin

cael

The Council for Adult & Experiential Learning
Chicago

KENDALL/HUNT PUBLISHING COMPANY
4050 Westmark Drive   Dubuque, Iowa 52002

cael

The Council for Adult & Experiential Learning
243 South Wabash Avenue, Suite 800
Chicago, Illinois 60604

All photographs by Victor J.E. Merritt, Visual Images & Concepts;
Boston, Massachusetts

To Ezra

who has helped in more ways than he is aware and who remains my best "rooter."

CONTENTS

Preface xiii
Introduction xvii

Chapter 1
Going Back to School 1

The Adult on Campus 1
What Colleges and Universities Are Doing for Adults 5
Experiential Learning 6
Learning Styles 7
Basic Skills for College Work 9
Next Steps 10

Chapter 2
Profiles of Five Adult Learners 11

The Value of Prior Learning Assessment 21

Chapter 3
Life and Career Planning: Making Informed Decisions 23

The Importance of Life and Career Planning 23
Defining Your Career Goals 26
Values Assessment 28
Skills Assessment 32
Transferable Skills 36
Resources for Career Planning 36
Developing Your Own Action Plan 38
A First Step 41

Chapter 4
Choosing the Right School: A Consumer's Guide to Postsecondary Education 43

Musts and Wants 44
How Schools and Colleges Work 46
Independent Learning 48
Learning to "Speak College" 51
Credit versus Non-Credit Study 53
Getting the Information You Need 53
Using College Catalogs 55
Follow-Up Activities 59
Hedging Your Bets 60
A Note of Caution 61

Chapter 5
Prior Learning Assessment: Getting Credit for What You Know 63

The Adult as an Accomplished Learner 64
You as a Learner 64
The Background of PLA Programs 67
Why PLA Programs are Important 68

Chapter 6
Some Methods Institutions Use to Evaluate Your Prior Learning 71

College Transcripts 72
Articulation Agreements 74
Credit by Examination 74
Credit for the Completion of Evaluated Programs 77
Credit for Professional Licenses or Certificates 79
Sample Applications of Assessment Methods 79

Chapter 7
Portfolio-Assisted Assessment 83

What Is a Portfolio? 84
Parts of the Portfolio 85
Identification and Definition of Prior Experiential Learning 85
College-Level Learning 98
The Essay or Narrative 101
Documenting Your Skills and Knowledge 103
Determining Your Credit Request 116
Organizing Your Portfolio 123
Submitting Your Portfolio 128
Faculty Evaluation 129
The Transcript 130

Chapter 8
Surviving and Thriving in College 131

Getting the Feel of the Campus 132
Managing Your Time 135
Creating a Support System 141
Money Matters 145
Developing Good Study Habits 148
Troubleshooting 155
Not All of a College Education Occurs in the Classroom 157

Appendix A
Ten Standards for Quality Assurance in Assessing Learning for Credit 159

Appendix B
Useful Books for Career Planning 161

Appendix C
General Skills List 163

Appendix D
Independent Learning Opportunities 167

Appendix E
Assessment Resources 171

Appendix F
Prior Learning Checklist 177

Appendix G
Learning Assessment Worksheet 181

Appendix H
Documentation Worksheet 185

Appendix I
Study Tips 187

Appendix J
Colleges and Universities with Prior Learning
Assessment Programs 191

Glossary 219

Index 227

PREFACE TO THE
——————— THIRD EDITION ———————

Experience is the best teacher.

A new edition of any book raises questions, especially when the subject is, like prior learning assessment, somewhat less subject to change than genome theory or rocket science. Have there been significant changes in the field that readers should know about? Is there new information about the availability of PLA to which students and practitioners should have access? Are there compelling reasons for readdressing the issues dealt with in the previous edition?

In the case of *Earn College Credit for What You Know*, the answer to all of these questions is "yes." Since publication of the second edition in 1992, there is new information about PLA techniques and practices. Business and professional groups have been pioneering new uses to which PLA can be put. There are new groups of people for whom PLA may be a valuable tool. A few colleges and universities previously listed as providing comprehensive PLA services no longer do so, but many more have entered the field. There are new sources of information about testing, evaluation, and career guidance, new addresses and phone numbers for older sources.

In the five years since publication of the second edition, adult learning has continued to assume more importance in this country as well as around the world. Recognizing that in a rapidly changing economy jobs demand continually updating old skills and developing new ones, people must now assume that they will go in and out of a formal learning mode throughout their careers. Lifelong learning has thus evolved from a fine sounding phrase to a widely recognized reality, and we have begun to pay more attention to independent or self-directed learning. As the population ages, we have also begun to recognize that there is a new generation of older adults, 65 to 95 or more, who in their "retirements" are continuing to learn both formally and informally in areas that support their aspirations for a healthier, more productive, more useful and satisfying old age. For them, too, prior learning assessment is a way of confirming their continuing growth and development.

Adoption of prior learning assessment ideas and methods by other countries in Europe and the Pacific have led to expanded educational roles for the PLA process that both include and go beyond the boundaries of colleges and universities. Moreover, as the number of working adults who are going back to school increases, the variety and types of learnings which they present for assessment have broadened and led to consideration of new issues and new practices.

In a rapidly changing economy, it is now widely recognized that further education is crucial to most working adults for whom progress on the career ladder is tied to their acquisition of new skills and competencies. For many people, a significant portion of these new skills and competencies has been acquired on the job, and it is critical that there be ways of measuring, evaluating, and possibly awarding credit for them, even outside the academic context. One response to this need has been more general acceptance of portfolio-assisted assessment as a flexible way of enabling adults to pull together diverse learnings into a coherent document. Increased importance is being given to evaluation of privately sponsored training programs and recommendation of credit for participation in them.

While the second edition of the book is still valid and full of useful information, a third edition has given me an opportunity to respond to some of the questions readers and professionals involved in assessment have asked and to include more information about how adults can manage the shoals and pitfalls of going back to school. This edition has new sections on experiential learning, independent learning, and learning styles, as well as expanded information on career and academic decision-making and study skills.

The appendices have been updated and expanded to include: a new bibliography of career planning materials (appendix B); a revised list of schools offering independent learning opportunities (appendix D); new and updated information on testing programs and assessment, including fax numbers, e-mail and website addresses (appendix E); and a revised list of study tips (appendix I).

Perhaps the most important change is in appendix J, in which the state-by-state listing of those colleges and universities which currently have comprehensive assessment programs has been totally revised, based on a current CAEL national survey. Here you will find listed institutions in every state in the country that offer some form of prior learning assessment.

As always, there are a host of colleagues and friends who have been crucial to the making of this edition. Primary among them was the late Marty Hanifin, a good friend who was unfailingly helpful and skilled at removing obstacles. Thanks are also due to his successor at CAEL, Stephen Nunes, who has been a friendly voice on the other end of my phone line, upbeat and responsive to my requests for information, resources, and advice. Diana Bamford-Rees is another member of the CAEL family who has been supportive and wise in directing me to new information about current PLA practices.

Two highly professional practitioners of PLA, Elana Michelson of Empire State College and Denise Hart of Fairleigh Dickinson University, kept me *au courant* with what is happening, and were available to discuss new issues and theoretical approaches to PLA.

As always, I must acknowledge my considerable indebtedness to Morris Keeton, mentor and friend, whose thinking and writing about the philosophical and pragmatic bases of prior learning assessment and whose continuing concern for issues of quality and fairness have provided the foundations on which all of us build. Thanks also to Urban Whitaker, the second of the two wise men, whose ideas grow younger and more flexible with the years, and who always stimulates me to new ways of thinking about PLA.

A lot of other people have been helpful and supportive. For whatever is right about this book I must also thank: Lynn Schroeder, my original editor for the second edition, whose criticism and suggestions were given, no matter how thorny the issue, cheerfully and with maximum encouragement (she's a great psychologist as well as editor); those who gathered and collated the results of the newest College PLA Survey; and, finally, those practitioners who took the time to answer my lengthy queries about how to improve the book: Sharyn Boornazian, Cambridge College; Nancy Lile, Northwestern College; Dale Mort, Lancaster Bible College; Larry Seid, Regis University; Karen Singleton, Chatham College; Ruth Silvestro, Rio Salado Community College; Linda Tibbets, Antioch University; and Wayne Virsig, Virginia State University.

For errors of fact or judgment, I take full responsibility, but then I, too, am an adult learner, and learning never ends.

Introduction

One must learn
By doing the thing; for though you
think you know it
You have no certainty, until you try.

Sophocles

This book is written for the millions of adults in the United States and elsewhere who know that high school graduation is nearer to the beginning of learning than to the end. It is written for all those who have continued to learn and grow since leaving school, those who have developed their job-related skills and competencies, or kept up with political events, or pursued a sport or craft or hobby, or just read and listened and observed and tried new things because they enjoyed knowing more about their world.

This book is being written for you who had the curiosity to pick it up off a bookstore or library shelf.

Basically the purpose of the book is to help you, the reader, think about what you have learned in your life so far, whether some of that learning may be appropriate for assessment for college credit, and how to go about earning that credit.

This book has three basic aims. The first is to convince you that you are a learner. You have always been a learner. You have been learning since you were first able to grasp a rattle or tie your own shoes or say your first words. You have learned at home and in school, at work and in church, on your own and with the help of parents, friends, spouses, teachers, and mentors. You have learned from newspapers and magazines and books, from radio and television, from computers and VCRs, in factories and offices, in museums and churches, on the Internet and CD Roms. You have learned while working in your garden, or taking care of your children, or managing your neighbor's campaign for City Council, or rebuilding the engine of your 1965 Pontiac GTO.

The second aim of this book is to help you get credit for those components of your learning that are similar to what is taught in colleges. Everything you have learned is valuable. The sum of your learning is what makes you a competent worker, a caring family member and friend, an informed citizen, or a "hot shot" tennis player. But some of what you have learned on your own may also be equivalent to what is being taught in colleges and universities. That is, the knowledge you gained from your job in an automobile plant may approximate what you might have learned in some or all of a program in automotive technology. And the volunteer work you've done with an environmental group, plus your reading on the environment, may have resulted in learnings that are very similar to what is taught in a course on ecology.

You *are* what you have experienced and learned, and everything that you have learned has enriched your life. Acquiring learning on your own is a significant accomplishment that should make you proud. Whether or not some of that learning will prove to be comparable to what is taught in colleges and whether it will also be appropriate to your educational goals or a degree program will be part of your process of discovery as you go through this book and as you talk to academic and assessment advisers in the schools.

Our third aim is to help you make a successful transition back to school.

The first four chapters of the book will: 1) give you an idea of the extent and reasons for the extraordinary movement of adults onto college campuses and discuss experiential learning and learning styles; 2) present the lifelong learning profiles of five adults who are about to go back to school; 3) encourage you to think about your own goals in seeking further education and to set up an action plan to achieve those goals; and, 4) urge you to be a *smart consumer* of education, so that your choices of schools, programs, courses, and activities will reflect your own needs, interests and values.

In chapter 5 you will be looking at all aspects of prior learning assessment, why it is useful to adults, how it works, and, most important, how it can work for you. You will also be encouraged to begin to think about yourself as a learner.

In chapters 6 and 7 you will find out how to have the learning that you have accomplished on your own assessed for college credit, whether through transfer of transcript credit, tests, evaluation of non-college courses you have taken, or portfolio-assisted assessment.

Finally, in chapter 8, you will read about some of the issues adults encounter upon returning to school, and get some help in devising strategies to cope with these issues.

Throughout the book, you will be encouraged to understand and respect the learning and skills you have acquired. You will also be assisted in defining those skills and learnings in ways that will make it easier to equate them with what is taught in colleges and universities. The text covers the various ways schools go about "assessing" learning, and concentrates on helping you to present the case for the validity of your own learning in the strongest way possible.

Above all, this book should give you respect for yourself as a learner, and should deepen the meaning for you of the phrase "Learning never ends."

Earn College Credit for What You Know is written in accord with CAEL's standards of good practice in the assessment of learning for credit (see appendix A), and is dedicated to helping you receive fair and valid recognition for what you have learned.

CHAPTER 1

Going Back to School

Very late in life, when he was studying geometry, some one said to Lacydes, "Is it then a time for you to be learning now?"
"If it is not," he replied, "when will it be?"

Diogenes

▲ The Adult on Campus

So you're thinking about going back to school. If you're like most other adults, you're probably also worrying about going back to school. "How will it feel to be the oldest in the class?" "Am I too old to learn?" "Have I forgotten how to study?" "Will the 19-year-olds resent my being there?" "Why am I doing this anyway?"

Well, relax. One of the most important trends today is the movement of adults like yourself back to the campus, and it is transforming the face of higher education across the country. First, more

One of the most important trends today is the movement of adults like you going back to campus, and it is transforming the face of higher education across the country.

adults are in school today than ever before, and the number is still climbing. You won't be the only one on campus with gray hair and a mortgage or a sink full of dirty dishes waiting for you in the kitchen. Right now, on the average college campus, about two out of five students are combining their studies with working at full-time jobs or caring for young children (or both) and carrying on other family and community responsibilities. More than one-third of college students today are over 25 years old, and in community colleges, the average age of students is over 38. On most campuses, adults predominate in evening and weekend classes to the extent that one traditional age learner apologized to his classmates because he was the only one who wasn't paying his own tuition. This trend, which started about 20 years ago, shows no signs of slackening; a study by the U.S. Department of Education[1] projects that by the year 2003, 6,654,000 adults over 25 will be enrolled in colleges, full- or part-time, making up 41 percent of the total enrollees in higher education. Of those older students, 41 percent are projected to be men, 59 percent women. Indeed, if one looks at just part-time enrollments, by 1998, over 74 percent will be older students. On a straight head count basis, full-time and part-time, the number of adults over the age of 22 attending college classes already (1997) exceeds that of younger students, 60 to 40 percent.

The graying of the American population as the nation's average age grows steadily higher, the demands of rapidly changing technologies for trained workers, the average person's realization that there is more to life than a job, beer, and television, and the desire to improve the quality of our lives are all factors in the return of adults to schools. These influences are contributing to dramatic changes on college campuses.

Second, you are not too old to learn. A number of studies confirm that on average, maturity and experience give older students certain advantages over younger students that enable them to more than hold their own academically. Indeed, most college faculty have found that the presence of mature students in their classes is intellectually challenging both to them and to the other students, and

---

[1] *Projections of Education Statistics to 2003.* Washington, D.C.: National Center for Education Statistics, 1992 (NCES 92-218), p. 27.

significantly raises the level of discourse. If you still think you're too old to learn, you may meet some members of the class of 1940 who will change your mind. Recent research on the rapidly grow-ing population of elderlearners, 65 and over, is very encouraging about their ability to retain unimpaired cognitive functioning well into their eighties and even nineties.

Third, if your vision of college is derived from movies in which attractive young people devote most of their energies to going to football games and dances and spend more time worrying about dates than studying, it's time to update that image. Or if you think that college is a place where ancient professors lecture from ancient notes about boring subjects that have no relevance to the real world, that perception also needs revising. The average college campus to-day is a cosmopolitan place where people of diverse ages, races, and ethnic backgrounds pursue their individual academic and career goals in an atmosphere that is increasingly responsive to their vary-ing needs, backgrounds, and learning styles. While most colleges still offer the challenge of competitive sports and the potential for an active social life, those that recognize the changing nature of their students also try to accommodate the needs and interests of part-time adult students who have multiple commitments to jobs, fami-lies, and economic survival. You are as likely to find a parent train-ing group as a sorority on campus and to find groups addressing environmental concerns, local traffic, recycling policy, and interna-tional peacekeeping efforts attended by people of all ages. Profes-sors have grown accustomed to being challenged in class by stu-dents who are older than they are, and most of them welcome the interest and commitment of their adult students.

If you were to attend the typical college graduation today, you would find in attendance not only parents and grandparents, but also children and grandchildren, proudly watching as their own mothers, fathers, and grandparents receive their diplomas.

Perhaps some of your anxiety about going back to school is based on your earlier experiences. If your memories of being in a class-room include boredom, repression, fear of making mistakes or get-ting bad grades, unsympathetic teachers, too many other students or too many rules, then keep in mind that colleges and universities today are different from these memories, and, more important, you are different.

Exercise 1-1 provides a way to allow you to think about "then and now," to understand that how you reacted to school when you were a teenager may be very different from how you would react today.

▼ **Exercise 1-1:** Then and Now

Draw a line down the middle of a blank piece of paper. On the left side of the line, put down some phrases that represent **"THEN"**—how you used to feel about school, the good and the bad. Remember the fun you had with your friends, the trouble you had with algebra or Spanish, your longing to be outdoors playing ball rather than sitting for hours in class, your worries about whether you should wear loafers or sneakers . . .

On the right side of the line, put down some words or phrases that reflect you **"NOW"**—you as an adult who has had a number of significant life experiences and has gained a measure of self-confidence from involvement in work and family and community activities—you as an adult who has chosen to go to school. Think about what school can do for you; the level of your adult commitment to learning; your present hopes and fears; the changes in your life that going back to school will create.

Put the piece of paper away for a few days, then take it out again, and after rereading it, add whatever additional thoughts you have had on either side of the line.

▲

Most adults find that this exercise opens their minds to some profound differences between schooling "then and now" and helps them resolve some of their doubts about returning to the classroom.

▲ What Colleges and Universities Are Doing for Adults

Although teaching 18 to 22-year-old traditional students is still an important part of a college or university's job, **the adult student represents its future.** Institutions of higher education used to "tolerate" adult students; they now welcome them. They used to segregate adults in separate classes, programs, or units; they now "mainstream" them. They used to consider themselves 9-to-5 institutions; they now hold evening and weekend classes. Some of them also provide child care, have special counselors trained to help older students with financial, academic, or career issues, offer financial aid packages specifically for adults, encourage adult support groups, and in general are moving toward a more flexible, more individualized way of dealing with the new reality that *ours is a learning society and all of us are lifelong learners.*

Prior learning assessment programs were to some extent adopted by higher education as a means of attracting older, more experienced men and women. These programs represent recognition that most people are engaged in informal learning activities throughout their lives and come back to the classroom with a background of experiential learning that makes them better students. Colleges have found that if they recognize such learning through fair and reliable evaluation procedures and award college credit when it is deserved, they can enhance the educational experience for their adult students and motivate them to continue learning.

▲ Experiential Learning

Mark Twain once remarked that "a man who carries a cat by the tail learns something he can learn in no other way." He was talking about the power of experiential learning.

Much of the learning that adults have acquired is "experiential," that is, it is learning created by the transformation of experience through the process of involvement, perception, and understanding that goes on as we work, play, marry, rear children, pursue hobbies, and develop relationships. To an extent all learning is experiential. In most classrooms the dissemination of theoretical or cognitive knowledge is accompanied by opportunities for students to test that knowledge by applying it to issues in their own personal, civic, ethical, or political lives, in laboratory experiments, and in subjective and critical analysis that matches theory against perceived reality.

Moreover, institutionally-sponsored experiential learning has a long and honorable history. For hundreds of years men and women have engaged in apprenticeships in the trades, clinical internships in medicine, practice teaching in education. Many schools' degree programs include a "practicum" which means that as part of the learning process, students are placed in a professional, business, organizational, or other setting in which the knowledge, skills, and competencies they've acquired in the classroom are augmented (and often transformed) by their immersion in the hands-on experience of actually working with colleagues and clients or out in the field.

Experiential learning is a critical element in the process of developing a multidimensional individual. The transformation of experience into learning is the true university of adulthood. What you have learned through experience, whether or not it is translated to credits and credentialling by the process of prior learning assessment, is the most important learning you have acquired.

▲ Learning Styles

Although all of us are learners throughout our lives, our learning styles can be very different. The following story about two brothers illustrates how our learning styles affect how we go about acquiring new knowledge and skills.

> After years of living in city apartments, two brothers, Jeff and Sam, moved to a home in the suburbs on a half-acre of land. Both had always wanted a garden, but neither had any experience of growing anything beyond a potted philodendron or a scraggly cactus.
>
> Jeff immediately introduced himself to their new next door neighbor, Mr. Ling, whose garden he admired. For the next few months he worked side by side with Mr. Ling, learning which tools he would need, how to prepare the soil, how to plant, when to water and feed, and why mulching is important. He spent long hours in the garden, watching Mr. Ling closely, questioning him about what he didn't understand, and becoming quite skilled in handling the plants. In the fall, Mr. Ling encouraged Jeff to harvest some of his vegetables for himself.
>
> Meanwhile, Sam went about learning to garden in a very different way. He sent away for a number of plant and seed catalogs, which he pored over during the winter in order to learn the names, habits, and soil and sun requirements of a variety of vegetables and flowers. He also subscribed to a gardening magazine and took a short course on plant diseases at the local agricultural extension college.

By the time spring arrived, Sam had planned their whole garden on paper, sent away for seeds, purchased the tools that were listed as best buys in a consumer's guide and sat back patiently to wait for April. Meanwhile, Jeff had planted tomato, marigold, and impatiens seeds in egg carton containers and had started them under a special light that he installed in the basement.

Jeff looked over Sam's plan and, remembering how clumsy he had felt tiptoeing between the rows in Mr. Ling's garden, suggested that they leave more space in their garden. He also made some changes in the kinds of vegetables they would grow, having observed that root vegetables did not do well in their clay soil.

In late March when the brothers proudly brought home their first major piece of garden equipment, a Rototiller™, Sam immediately sat down to read the owner's manual, while Jeff tore open the carton and began trying to fit the components together. They both laughed when they realized that once again they were acting out their different learning styles.

Jeff and Sam are both intelligent men, capable of learning complex skills and absorbing a great deal of sophisticated information. But Jeff's preferred learning styles are observation and experimentation. He typically wants to get his hands dirty. Sam's preferred learning styles are reading and reflection. He wants to understand the theory behind something before he tries it out. Together they could really create a terrific garden.

Experiential learning theory, as conceptualized by David Kolb, sees the learning process as a four-stage cycle: concrete experience; observation and reflection; formation of abstract concepts and generalizations; and testing implications of concepts in new situations. Immediate, concrete experience (working in the garden) is the basis for observation and reflection (realizing that the carrots are not growing well in a clay soil); this observation leads to the formation of abstract concepts and generalizations (root vegetables need a sandier soil); and finally to testing the implications of concepts in new situations (in this case, deciding to grow above ground vegetables); which in turn circles back to the concrete experience of doing so the next season. The learning cycle is circular and can be entered at any point. For some (Sam), the formation of abstract concepts and generalizations is the favored entry point. For others (Jeff), concrete experience is the primary way into the cycle.

A person's preferred learning style is not necessarily limiting, however. All of us have developed cross-over skills which enable us to learn in a variety of situations and in a variety of ways: from learning to ski by just getting out there and stumbling around until we're able to stay upright and negotiate turns; from talking to friends about the candidates for office and reflecting on what they say; from reading books or journals that help us form abstract concepts; from taking care of a neighbor's baby and observing its actions; from testing out different bait to see which the fish prefer.

Over the course of our lives, most of us develop learning styles that emphasize some learning abilities over others. It's a good idea to get to know your own preferred learning styles. It may help you understand why you are more comfortable in the library than in the laboratory, or why you like to work on a group project rather than alone. But don't let your learning style preference be a limitation. One of the great things about being a learner is the opportunity it provides not only to increase your knowledge and skills but to broaden the number of ways in which you can learn.[2]

▲ Basic Skills for College Work

Although most adults are better learners than they were in high school, some who didn't get a firm grounding in the basic skills during their grade school and high school years—who didn't learn to read or write or do basic mathematical computations with ease—must face the possibility that they may need help in developing these skills before they can progress satisfactorily in college work. If you suspect that your basic skills need improvement, you should face this realistically and find out what kind of support the college of your choice can give you. Most schools offer (or even require) diagnostic basic skills tests, and they also have special courses or workshops or tutoring programs to help you improve your verbal, math and reasoning skills. Free or low cost basic skills help is also available to taxpayers through local school districts or through local community colleges. There is no disgrace in attending these

---

[2] If you're interested in reading more about learning styles, the following books will be helpful: Kolb, David A., *Learning Style Inventory*. McBer & Co., 1976. Claxton, Charles S., *Learning Styles*. Washington: American Association for Higher Education, 1978.

classes or workshops; there *is* disgrace in trying to hide your lack of skills, thereby endangering your ability to succeed in college. You owe it to yourself to eliminate as many barriers to success as possible. Don't stand in your own way.

▲ Next Steps

Let's assume that you're very comfortable about going back to school. Is it time to fill out an application and register? Perhaps. It's time to apply for admission if:

- ▲ you're fairly clear about why you're going back to school and what you want out of further education;
- ▲ you know which colleges have the courses and programs you need;
- ▲ you have information about how responsive each of those colleges is to adult students;
- ▲ you've thought seriously about what you have learned on your own and about whether that learning may qualify for college credit; and
- ▲ you understand the changes in your life style that going back to college may entail.

The balance of this book will help you to think about and understand these issues, to ferret out the information you need, and to make informed decisions that will enable you to fulfill your hope of increasing your own potential through returning to learning— whether this means taking a few courses, completing a certificate program, or earning a degree.

2

Profiles of
Five Adult Learners

Only so much do I know, as I have lived.
Ralph Waldo Emerson

In the five case histories that follow, you will get to know some actual adult learners, all of them interesting people who may be similar to people you know—or even to you. These men and women come from different kinds of backgrounds, have lived very different lives, and have developed diverse interests, skills, and learnings. What they have in common is that they have reached a crucial point in their lives, a point when further education makes sense if they are to move on personally and in their careers.

In later chapters, we will refer to these people and look at how they approached and resolved many of the decisions you will be facing as you contemplate going back to school. And you will discover how Scott, Joan, Dorene, Max, and Anna chose career paths, schools, and programs and went about preparing to have their prior learning assessed for college credit.

Scott is 46 years old and works for a large lumber company. He has become both a skilled mechanic and an accomplished wood worker.

▲ Scott A.

Scott A. is 46 years old. Since he was 16 he has worked at various jobs for a paper company. He has planted trees, cut timber, transported it down the river, and done a number of other jobs, both skilled and non-skilled, that are part of logging. He is also a good mechanic and is the one everyone turns to when a tractor or skidder or giant saw malfunctions.

Thinking that he might like a change, Scott spent a few years on transfer to the company's paper mill in a nearby city. While he learned a lot about the technology of paper making, that experience taught him that he would be miserable if he had to spend all his working days cooped up in a factory. He needs the feeling of freedom he gets from working outdoors.

Scott never graduated from high school. This began to bother him when his own children reached high school, so two years ago he started to attend evening school to study for a G.E.D. (General Education Development exam; the G.E.D. is equivalent to a high school diploma). He passed the test easily, and his experience has given him the courage to think about going on to college.

For the past few years, Scott has worked as first assistant to Rich, a unit manager with a degree in forestry. Rich has encouraged Scott to take advantage of the company's pre-paid tuition plan to go back to school so that he can advance into a crew leader position. This prospect appeals to Scott because he no longer feels as strong or agile as he once was, and his present job involves physical risk. Scott sometimes thinks about early retirement, but he would need to earn money to supplement his reduced pension and has begun to think about alternative careers.

In his leisure time, Scott does a lot of bass fishing. He also belongs to a Bible study group and is an accomplished woodworker who has designed and made much of the furniture in his home.

Scott has already made initial inquiries about local educational opportunities and has found a community college that not only offers an associate degree in forestry but will assess his prior learning for possible credit.

Joan is a 42-year-old divorced mother of two children. After years of experience as a volunteer at a local art museum, her short term goal is to complete the college degree in art she began 18 years ago.

▲ Joan B.

Joan B. grew up in a large city in the East, spending much of her time during high school cutting classes so that she could visit museums and galleries and see the latest foreign films. Although she learned a lot about art, her school grades were low and she could only get into a "second rate" college, which she left after the first semester.

Against her family's wishes, Joan married when she was 19 and had two children by the time she was 21. Because her husband was fairly well to do, she didn't work outside her home. Later she trained to become a volunteer docent (guide) at the local art museum, worked with the city's committee to build an arts center, and teamed up with a friend to write, direct, and produce a film on artists in the city.

Joan's husband became an alcoholic, and, when drunk, a wife abuser. Although she spent many years trying to help him by supporting his involvement in Al Anon and other counseling programs, Joan finally left him when his addiction worsened and he began to abuse the children. Although Joan receives some child support for her 15 and 17-year-old sons, she gets no money for herself. Her long range plans are to get a graduate degree in business so that she can pursue a career as an administrator of arts programs. Her immediate goal is to complete the college degree she began 18 years ago.

A local college has a prior learning assessment program, and Joan is beginning to think about what college level learning she has acquired on her own.

▲ Dorene G.

Dorene G. went straight from high school into a secretarial job with a major communications company. She had learned typing, filing, and shorthand in her high school vocational education program, and since joining the company has become proficient in using computers, has taken a company course in a computerized spreadsheet program, and has taught herself word processing. She is the office expert in word processing and is responsible for teaching the program to new secretaries. She has also taught herself desktop publishing and has designed and produced on her own the new

Dorene, now 27 years old, went straight from high school into a secretarial position, where she eventually became proficient in office skills and several computer software applications.

company personnel forms and a personnel benefits brochure. She was very proud when the president told her supervisor that she had done a more elegant job than the professional designer who had done the previous brochure.

In the past, Dorene was closely affiliated with her union and was active in organizing and contract arbitration. She has taken a number of union-sponsored courses in labor relations and labor history.

Because the grandparents who raised Dorene were born in Puerto Rico, she grew up bilingual, speaking English and Spanish. She has made a few trips to Puerto Rico to visit relatives and has become politically involved in the Puerto Rican movement for statehood, on which she has read a great deal and for which she gives speeches and writes articles. She also reads fiction by Puerto Rican and other Latin American authors in the original Spanish and collects native South American crafts.

Dorene's ambition is to move up to a management position in her present company, but she believes she needs further credentials. She would like to take advanced work in computer science, but she hesitates to commit herself to going for a degree at this time because she hopes to get married and have children in a few years. She also doesn't want to take courses in subjects she thinks she already knows, which is why she is investigating the possibility of prior learning assessment.

▲ Max W.

Max W. works for a major automobile manufacturer, where he manages the parts warehouse in a truck division. Prior to being trained by the company for that job, he had worked on the production line doing welding, painting, and assembly. During the Vietnam War he spent two years in the U.S. Coast Guard, where he was in charge of communications for his company.

Max is a single parent, raising two small children by himself, and in his spare time he and his girlfriend are active in a black community youth group working with troubled school drop-outs. He also plays the trumpet and is interested in both jazz and classical music.

Max's company provides support for going back to school, and Max says, "It's my time now." He finished a CLEP preparation

Max, a 35-year-old single parent of two young children, works for a major automobile manufacturer as manager of the parts warehouse. In his spare time, he is active in a community youth group for troubled school drop-outs.

course and then took five general CLEP tests (see chapter 6, pp. 74–75) for which he was awarded 30 credits toward an associate's degree. Before committing himself to a college program, he wants to get a rough picture of how much additional credit he might be able to earn through prior learning assessment.

▲ Anna P.

Until her recent 50th birthday, Anna P. never wanted to be anything but a wife and mother. She married her childhood sweetheart right after high school and had four children. While they were growing up, she became interested in child psychology and child development. Anna read many books on the subject and attended courses on parenting and child care at her church and through the continuing education classes offered at her local high school. After her mother died of cancer, she also became active in the local cancer society, running their fund-raising campaign for three consecutive years. During that time she was responsible for recruiting part-time volunteers, scheduling and managing their time, assigning their duties, and planning and coordinating all of the group's activities.

Anna's leisure pursuits include gourmet cooking and baking, for which she is locally famous. She is frequently asked to help cater church and community events and has taken a number of non-credit courses in Chinese, French, and Near Eastern cooking.

Anna reads a great deal, mostly novels by such nineteenth century authors as Charles Dickens, Anthony Trollope, and George Eliot. She has also read biographies of these authors and has begun to branch out into reading critical studies of their work.

Now that her children are either away at college or preparing for it, Anna is wondering what she wants to do with the rest of her life. A friend suggested that she might start a catering business, but Anna is worried about her lack of business experience. She is thinking about going to college for a business degree, but can't imagine spending the next four years doing that on a full time basis. She wonders if there is any way to shorten the time needed for a bachelor's degree.

Anna, who recently turned 50, studied a great deal about child psychology and child development while raising her four children. While at home, she also became a gourmet cook, for which she has become well known in her community.

▲ The Value of Prior Learning Assessment

All five of these people are at a stage of life in which a change of some sort is in process or is anticipated. Scott wants to position himself to get a better job in his company now, but he is also looking forward to developing skills that will let him earn a living if he takes early retirement. Joan needs to turn her volunteer activities into a paid career so that she can support her family. Dorene wants to move from a secretarial to a management position. Max wants to go to school to become a more rounded, better educated person. ("It's my time now.") And Anna finds that as her full-time job as a mother is coming to an end, it's time to broaden her horizons beyond home and family.

For all five of these people, further schooling seems to be a point of entry for moving on to the next phase of their lives. And all five of them have already accumulated at least some learning that may be similar to that which they could have acquired in a college setting.

For all five people, prior learning assessment will:

▲ validate the worth of learning they have achieved on their own;

▲ demonstrate to them what they still need to learn in order to achieve their personal, career, or academic goals;

▲ shorten the time necessary to earn a college degree;

▲ save them money by lessening the number of courses they need to take;

▲ enhance their pride and self-esteem for what they have accomplished as learners; and

▲ make them aware that learning is truly a lifelong process, **that learning never ends**.

3

Life and Career Planning: Making Informed Decisions

All experience is an arch to build upon.

Henry Adams

The purpose of this chapter is to help you think about your life, career, and academic goals in the context of a rational and realistic career planning process; to engage you in some self-assessment exercises that will help you to understand your own values, interests, and skills; and to introduce you to the career planning resources in your community.

▲ The Importance of Life and Career Planning

Why, you may be wondering, is there a chapter on life and career planning in a book on prior learning assessment? What does this have to do with me and my desire to earn college credit?

There are a number of resources available to help you get the information you need as you go through the process of career planning.

There are a number of connections to be made between prior learning assessment and life and career planning. For one thing, you need to be able to look at your prior learning in the context of what you plan to study in college. Some components of your prior learning may be more relevant to your educational goals than others, and you will want to emphasize these. For example, if you plan to enter a four-year program in social work, the knowledge you gained as a child-care worker will be more closely related to your major than your ability to install telephone systems. Or if you plan to work toward a degree in computer science, you will probably wish to put more emphasis on your experience in computer programming than on your skills in fashion merchandising.[1] In any case, you will need to be able to demonstrate to your assessors that there are connections between your prior learning and what you wish to study.

To put it another way, although the learning for which you hope to get some credit may have taken place in the past, your reasons for assessment should be directed toward your future. If you are able to state your life goals specifically, you will be better able to make specific educational plans (including plans for prior learning assessment) to reach those goals.

Even if you think you are certain of why you are going back to school and what you plan to study there, you still might take some time to at least skim this chapter to see if any of its content applies to you. Situations change, the economy changes, our personal likes and dislikes change. Even if you have been through some life-planning exercises before, you will probably find it worthwhile to think about some of the issues raised in the following pages, to complete some of the self-assessment exercises, and to attempt to set down on paper your specific reasons for wanting to go back to school.

What do you want to be doing in five years? Ten years? Do you want to enter a new vocation or profession? Do you want to increase your competence in a skill you already have? Do you want to find a solution to a serious social or environmental problem? Do you want to enrich your retirement years? Do you want to acquire credentials for professional advancement? Do you want to change your routine and learn something entirely new? Answering these and

---

[1] Your learnings in fields other than your major (or concentration) may still be useful in fulfilling your electives (or general distribution) requirements.

other questions about your future will help you map out your educational objectives. It will also assist you in thinking about the learning you have already accomplished.

▲ Defining Your Career Goals

Exercise 3-1 will help you begin to define exactly why you're contemplating going back to school, what you hope to get out of it, and how to think about the issues of courses, programs, and degrees as they relate to your current job and future career or life goals.

▼ Exercise 3-1: Why Do You Want to Go Back to School?

Take a few minutes to think about this question; then write a brief statement about why you want to go to school. Be as specific as possible about your needs and interests and the decisions you have already made. The point of stating, as specifically as possible, your reasons for going back to school is to enable you to make intelligent, informed choices about your future: which school to attend, which programs or courses to take, whether it is in your interest to work toward a degree or not, and so forth.

Your first statement may be general, such as "I want to improve my job skills," or "I want to become a graphic artist," or "I want to help people," but if it is going to be helpful to you, you must try to refine it.

For example, Dorene G. (see her profile, chapter 2, p. 15), who works in an office where she uses the computer for word processing and spread sheets, wants to go to school to "learn more about computers." That's a fine beginning statement, but before it can serve as a guide to further choices, Doreen needs to think about some of the following:

▲ Does she want to "learn more about computers" to do something specific, like using a database management system?

▲ Is she interested in computers from the perspective of an engineer (how they work, how they are designed), a sociologist (what is the computer's effect on society), or a public health science specialist (what are the risks of prolonged exposure to a video display terminal)?

▲ Since she is hoping to advance to a management position in her present company, would it be to her advantage to earn a degree? If so, which degree?

▲ Would a certificate program in computer science or computer programming or management information science (MIS) answer her needs as well as would a degree?

▲ If her needs are specific, such as wanting to learn desktop publishing or spreadsheet analysis, could one or two courses give her the skills and information she wants?

These are the kinds of questions Dorene should ask herself before she tries to make final choices about schools, programs or courses.

What kinds of questions do you need to ask yourself that will enable you to make smart choices? It may be that you aren't able to be more specific at this time because you need more information or more time to think about it. You may even feel that you need to talk to a guidance counselor who can help you make decisions about your career and academic goals. That's OK. In fact, knowing that you don't know enough to make a good decision right now may be the most helpful outcome of this exercise. It may spur you on to get the information you need.

▲

Perhaps you are already very clear about your career goals. You may want to earn a certificate in paralegal studies so that you can move up from secretary in your present legal firm to a better paying, more professional job in that same firm. Or you may be planning to take a few courses in bookkeeping and business skills so you can get out of your present job selling cars and open a motorcycle repair shop with your brother-in-law. Or your plans may be to earn a bachelor's degree in agronomy as a first step toward getting a job in the U.S. Department of Agriculture. Or you may just want to take some writing courses so you can write your family's history.

It is important to understand that career planning does not necessarily mean career change. If you are happy or secure in your present job, you may or may not wish to change that job for another, even within the same organization. On the other hand, if your current job leaves you unfulfilled or feeling like a square peg in a round hole, you may wish to move on to something totally different or to develop a "second career" or hobby that will give you more personal satisfaction. In that case, you should be aware that every organization has career paths, opportunities to move to very different jobs or upward to more complex or more responsible jobs in the same general area. These paths are not always well publicized or clearly articulated, so you may have to piece information together from several sources to understand how they work. Just remember that you don't always have to switch companies in order to switch jobs.

To make informed decisions about your own career path, you should not only learn more about career opportunities that relate to your current job or to the field you want to study, you should also listen to the inner voice that tells you what values and interests you must satisfy if you are to be happy in your work life.

▲ Values Assessment

We are all different. June enjoys selling major kitchen appliances at the Acme Home Store. She enjoys meeting customers and discovering the best way to get and keep their interest. She enjoys learning about the technical aspects of her merchandise. She even enjoys the competition with other sales people in the store. Her best friend, Sherie, is much happier working in the back office at Acme. Sherie is uncomfortable with strangers, is not interested in technical information, and hates competition. She also feels that she lacks the stamina to stand on her feet on the sales floor all day long, and she doesn't want to work on Saturdays when her children are home from school. On the other hand, Sherie enjoys laying out Acme's newspaper ads, enjoys setting up business systems, and takes pride in her knowledge that she writes better business letters than anyone else in the firm.

Although both June and Sherie seem well matched for their current jobs, June's ambitions for more money and increased prestige have made her consider earning a degree in retailing. This will enable her to build on her present skills and put her in line for a career as buyer or sales manager. Ultimately June hopes to own her own store, so she also wants to develop some business and financial management skills.

Sherie, on the other hand, cares less about money than she does about having more leisure time to spend with her children and to work on her part-time job, illustrating children's books. Her goal is to find a career that will enable her to work at home while pursuing her artistic interests. This fall she plans to take a course in child development to enhance her parenting skills and a drawing workshop given by a famous illustrator to develop her creative talents. She hopes eventually to leave her present job and work full time at home as an illustrator.

Both women have become aware that their own values and interests are as important as their skills in determining their futures, and they are making their educational plans accordingly.

Exercise 3-2 provides an opportunity for you to begin thinking about your own values—what's really important to you—and about how those values are now or can be expressed in the work you do.

▼ Exercise 3-2: Assessing Your Values

Following is a list of values for you to consider. Some values will be more important to you than others. Some may not be very important at all. Rank these values from the most important (1) to least important (16).

To rank the values, imagine you have the world's worst job, a job where none of your values are fulfilled. If your employer offered you a chance to have one of your values fulfilled, which one would it be? What would be the next one? The next? Keep going until you have ranked all 16. Expect to change your mind several times before coming up with your final order. (Put the numbers in the left margin, and use a pencil so you can erase when you change your mind.)

Ranking Your Values

_____ ADVANCEMENT—A chance to advance in a career; to be promoted.

_____ LEARNING—A chance to learn new skills and knowledge.

_____ MONEY—Having a decent salary and benefits; a chance for overtime.

_____ RECOGNITION—Having your efforts appreciated; getting credit for a job well done; having your suggestions listened to.

_____ WORKING CONDITIONS—Having a pleasant work environment (not too hot, cold, dirty, noisy, crowded).

_____ RELATIONSHIPS—Having a good working rapport with your supervisor and co-workers; team spirit; companionship.

_____ HOURS—Having the work schedule you want (daytime, nighttime, weekdays, weekends, full-time, part-time, flex-time).

_____ SECURITY—Having a job that you can count on, even in hard times; a job from which you won't be laid off.

_____ CREATIVITY—A chance to think up new ideas, try new ways of doing things, figure out solutions to problems your own way.

_____ HELPING OTHERS—Working with people in ways that can have a positive effect on their lives.

_____ INDEPENDENCE—A chance to be your own boss; to make decisions on your own; to work without constant supervision.

_____ LEADERSHIP—An opportunity to inspire, plan or organize and oversee the work of others; supervise.

_____ VARIETY—A chance to do different kinds of work; not the same task over and over.

_____ PRESTIGE—A chance to do work that others respect; to do work you are proud of.

_____ LEISURE—Work which leaves you free to have time for yourself for relaxation, hobbies, etc.

_____ PEACE OF MIND—Work that gives you freedom from pressure, deadlines, anxiety, stress, etc.

_____ OTHER—Any other values that are important to you; that you care about.

_____

_____

Based on your own numbering of this list, rank your values below, in order of importance (most important near the top; less important near the bottom). Next to each value, indicate how satisfied or how dissatisfied you are with respect to it in your present job and what you hope for in your next job.

To fill out the third column, think about your critical values, those that must be present if you were to accept a job. The classic example is the person who can only work out of doors and will not accept office work no matter how high the salary or great the prestige. Can you imagine a kind of work that would allow you to express your own unique values? Is that the kind of work you are planning to study for when you return to school?

If your expressed values seem pretty far from your anticipated life's work, you may wish to talk to a career or educational counselor before making any further decisions.

Ranking Scale For Values Exercise

0—No problem. I am satisfied with things the way they are.
1—Some improvement would be nice, but I can live with things the way they are.
2—I don't like things the way they are. I want to do something about it.
3—I am very dissatisfied. I definitely want a change.

Rank	Value	Present Job	Next Job
1.	_____	_____	_____
2.	_____	_____	_____
3.	_____	_____	_____
4.	_____	_____	_____
5.	_____	_____	_____
6.	_____	_____	_____

Rank	Value	Present Job	Next Job
7.	_____	_____	_____
8.	_____	_____	_____
9.	_____	_____	_____
10.	_____	_____	_____
11.	_____	_____	_____
12.	_____	_____	_____
13.	_____	_____	_____
14.	_____	_____	_____
15.	_____	_____	_____
16.	_____	_____	_____

Note that the values at the top of the list are the most important to you. If some of them received a score of 2 or 3, you may want to consider holding out for greater satisfaction in these critical areas in your next job.

▲

Once you have begun to think seriously about your own values, you will take them into consideration whenever you are confronted with the need to make career choices or other life-style choices. Perhaps you have found that money is less important to you than your working conditions, or that you are willing to trade off prestige for peace of mind. These are critical issues that can lead to long-term satisfaction or dissatisfaction with your career, so don't ignore them. And don't discount the possibility that these values may change; they can shift depending upon your age and new interests. Some counselors recommend that people repeat a values exercise every few years to keep in touch with changes in their own needs.

▲ Skills Assessment

Skills are the things you do well, things for which you have talent or that you have learned to do. They may be related to your present job (typing, fixing machinery, selling, teaching) or they may be unrelated to it (entertaining, playing basketball, working with teenagers, singing). Most people possess 500–700 specific skills, most of which are marketable, so don't be modest about your own list. Put down as many skills as you can think of.

It may be helpful to think about your skills in terms of the following categories (see also the general skills list in appendix C):

Communications:
    Reading
    Writing
    Speaking
    Listening

Mathematical/Computational Skills

Intellectual:
    Ability to learn
    Analysis
    Synthesis
    Critical reasoning
    Scientific reasoning
    Problem solving

Interpersonal:
    Ability to get along with different kinds of people
    Leadership
    Negotiation
    Teamwork/working in groups
    Influencing

Physical:
    Specific sports skills
    Specific physical abilities

Personal:
    Creativity
    Self-development
    Persistence
    Motivation
    Planning
    Self-confidence

Professional or technical:
    Skills that enable one to do specific jobs—build things, fix things, manage things, etc.

A skills list was compiled by **Scott,** the man who works in the timber industry (see profiles, chapter 2, p. 13). His list is not complete, but he has made a good start at determining what skills he has already acquired in life.

Communications:
Reading comprehension (Scott enjoys reading the Bible, Bible commentary, mysteries, sports articles, and books)
Speaking (He leads a Bible study group, makes speeches to local organizations in support of sports for kids)
Listening (in order to facilitate discussion in the Bible study group, he must listen intently to what people say in order to respond appropriately)

Mathematical/computational:
Arithmetic
Algebra and plane geometry
Figuring board feet of lumber

Interpersonal:
Gets along well with logging manager and fellow workers
Is the one in the family to whom his brothers bring their problems
Has sustained a happy marriage for 12 years
Still close to old friends from high school

Physical:
Fishing
Bowling
Weight lifting

Professional or technical:
Woodworking
    finishing/refinishing
    basic carpentry
    furniture design
    furniture making
Mechanical skills
    Maintaining diesel engines, heavy machinery, boat motors
Applied electronics
    Fixing electric appliances
    Wiring, rewiring
Forestry
    Timbering, transporting
    Operating bull dozers, tractors, skidders
    Reforestation (planning/planting) skill

Once his counselor convinced Scott that he was not "bragging," he was able to extend the list far beyond what you see above, particularly in such areas as leadership, persistence, motivation, and self-development.

Anna (see profiles, chapter 2, p. 19), who is rather shy, had to be persuaded by a college counselor to even attempt to list her skills. Her initial list is quite different from Scott's, but also extensive.

Communications:
Reading (Anna has read extensively in child psychology and 19th century British fiction; she also reads two newspapers a day and subscribes to a number of cooking magazines.)
Listening (Anna says a good parent must know how to listen carefully.)
Speaking German (Anna's parents were refugees from Germany in World War II, and she learned the language in order to communicate better with them and other relatives.)

Mathematical/computational:
Household budgeting
Conversion of recipe ingredients from metric to U.S. measures, equivalents

Interpersonal:
Child care, child psychology
Making and keeping friends
Entertaining
Maintaining a happy, loving marriage

Physical Skills:
Aerobic dancing
Hiking

Professional or technical:
Basic cooking techniques
Basic baking techniques
Other cuisines (German, French, Chinese, Near Eastern)
Catering
    Portion control
    Buying in bulk
    Time management in the kitchen
Household management
Management of a nonprofit organization
    Planning skills
    Personnel management
    Administration

▼ **Exercise 3-3:** Your Skills

List your own skills on a separate piece of paper.

Do you use any of your skills in your present job?

How could you use your strongest skills more?

Are there any skill areas you'd like to develop more?

▲

▲ Transferable Skills

Remember, many of your skills are *transferable*, that is, they can be used with some modification in different situations. If you have shown an aptitude for simple arithmetic in your current job as a bookkeeper, you may find that you do well in other aspects of mathematics, in engineering, and possibly in science. Or if you are a competent truck driver with a "feel" for engines, you may do well in physics, mechanics, or engineering. Basic language skills—speaking, reading, writing, listening—are highly transferable in fields as diverse as selling, business management, journalism, and teaching, to name just a few. Homemaking skills may translate well to hospitality management, social work, dressmaking, or child care. In any case, your skills go with you through life and can greatly ease the transition from one mode of work to another.

Certainly, many of these skills will directly influence how well you do in further schooling. Whether they are appropriate for credit or not, they will make you a better learner and facilitate your success in college.

▲ Resources for Career Planning

Once you have formed some idea of your own interests, values and skills, you are better equipped to determine what kinds of work might capitalize on your strengths, fulfill your needs, and enable you to earn a better living. In a constantly changing labor market, you will also need information about the current availability of jobs in your area as well as the educational and experiential requirements for those jobs. There are a number of resources available to help you get the information you need as you go through the process of career planning.

1. Counselors at your local high school, the public library, or the college you are planning to attend.

2. Computerized "career information systems" such as SIGI-PLUS, Choices, or Discover for Adults (these may also be available at high schools, public libraries, and colleges).

3. Career counselors in the personnel department of your company or union.

4. Informational interviews with people holding the kinds of jobs in which you might be interested.

5. A computer database, "Guidance Information Services (GIS)," available in many schools and employment services, which has up-to-date information on the job outlook for different careers.

6. The *Dictionary of Occupational Titles* (DOT), available in most libraries. It is a classification of almost all the jobs that exist in the United States. The jobs are described in detail, and they are classified with groups of related jobs. *The Occupational Outlook* discusses the educational requirements and job outlook for almost as many jobs. The two books are cross-referenced so that they can be used together.

7. Books on the job market and on different careers in your geographic area; these forecasts are often published by the Department of Commerce in your own state. The librarian can help you find the best sources for information on any career-related subject. (See also appendix B.)

8. Professional journals with recent articles about the field. Almost every occupation has its own trade or professional journal. If you take the time to look through journals of some of the career fields you are interested in, you can learn a lot about future trends in those careers.

9. The Internet has become a rich source for career planning resources. You might start your search by using words such as "guidance," "career choices," "career information," "occupations," etc.

A creative way of going about the process of making career decisions is to **read the social trends.** The following seem to be well established trends in the United States:

- ▲ the population is aging;
- ▲ two-family earners are the norm;
- ▲ computers are common in the home;
- ▲ the Internet is becoming a primary source of information and communication; and
- ▲ the population is highly exercise and diet conscious.

Think about these trends for a few minutes. What social changes might they involve? What goods and services might older people and families with two incomes need? Does the increasing number of home computers suggest any new or expanded opportunities for jobs? Does the Internet offer different publishing possibilities? Does the expansion of health consciousness suggest any new career opportunities?

For example, both older people and working women are increasingly turning to fast foods or catered meals, creating a number of new jobs in the food industry. An older population combined with the expanded health consciousness of Americans is a strong factor in the growth of health-related industries. Many magazines and newspapers, carrying ads and product information, are now published on the Internet. And the increasing availability of computers (as well as phone answering machines and fax machines) has enabled thousands of people to carry on their work in their homes. These and many trends like them will have a dramatic impact on the kinds of jobs that will be available in this country over the next decade. They demand that you do some creative thinking about what opportunities may open up for you.

▲ Developing Your Own Action Plan

Your future isn't something that just happens to you. You can make it what you want it to be. But this takes planning. If you have read through this chapter and done the exercises, you should be ready to begin right now shaping your own future.

What you need is a plan, a plan designed by you, for you, that will keep you on track to get you where you want to go. Exercise 3-4 will help you formulate such a plan.

▼ **Exercise 3-4:** Your Own Action Plan

1. **Name:**

2. **My current career goals are:** (be as specific as you can)

   Short-term:

   Long-term:

3. **I need the following preparation for this career:**
   (This may include courses, degrees, licenses, certificates, union membership, experience, any requirements necessary to make yourself eligible for employment in the career of your choice.)

   _____

   _____

   _____

4. **My skills/interests:**

   a. job skills:

   b. talents and aptitudes:

   c. interests:

5. **My current education goals:**

   (e.g., enrolling in _____ school; doing independent study at _____; other_____).

   Short-term:

   Long-term:

6. **Action Plan:** (steps to achieve your career and education goals)

   a. _____

   b. _____

   c. _____

   d. _____

e. _____

f. _____

7. Actions I need to take immediately:
(e.g., finding out if the local college offers the specific program you need, writing for a transcript, talking to a career counselor, getting information about prior learning assessment at the university, applying for admission, enrolling for a course, etc.)

8. Actions I need to take within the next 3 months:

9. Timeline:
(Do a week-by-week, month-by-month, year-by-year outline of what you will do to accomplish your goals)

_____

_____

_____

10. Pledge: I will carry out this action plan to the best of my ability in order to achieve my own career/educational objectives.

Signed: _____

▲

Write out your action plan on a separate piece of paper, tape it above your desk or put it in a safe place where you will see it every day, and then **start working on it.**

Your action plan will be especially useful to you when planning your college program or thinking about career change. Be sure to take it with you when you have scheduled a meeting with your college advisor or counselor.

▲ A First Step

This chapter has been only an introduction to career planning, a first step in the process. The intention is to encourage you to think about your future creatively, to make some preliminary decisions, to define your goals, to find out what you need to accomplish to achieve those goals, and to set about translating goals into reality. Appendix B contains a list of books and other resources for career planning.

4

Choosing the Right School: A Consumer's Guide to Postsecondary Education

Where there is much desire to learn, there of necessity will be much arguing, much writing, many opinions; for opinion in good men is but knowledge in the making.

John Milton

By now you've thought about why you want to go to school and what you want to study, you've developed an action plan, and you're ready to begin. Right? Well, not quite. There are very important differences among schools, and choosing the one that is accessible to you and right for you is not always easy.

After all, you wouldn't buy a car or a washing machine without doing some research on which is the best model (and the best buy) for your needs, nor would you go on a vacation without finding out whether the sports activities you like are available, what the weather is likely to be, and how much it will cost in both time and money.

In some ways, choosing a school is similar to choosing a car, a washing machine, or a vacation spot; the more you know about the alternatives, the better chance you have of making a choice that will be right for you.

The point of this chapter is to help you become a **smart consumer** of postsecondary education, to learn how to identify the college or other kind of school that is right for you and that will meet your needs in terms of degrees offered, programs and courses available, scheduling, accessibility, services, and so forth. The following pages cover:

▲ how colleges and universities work

▲ their special vocabulary (some people call it jargon)

▲ the advantages of degree and non-degree study

▲ nontraditional alternatives

▲ the kinds of questions you should ask about the schools you are considering

▲ the nature of your own demands on a school, both negotiable and nonnegotiable

▲ how to find the information you need to make intelligent decisions

▲ ways to "hedge your bets"

▲ Musts and Wants

Let's begin by thinking about what is most important to you in choosing a school. Exercise 4-1 will help you define what you must demand of a college. It lists some of the important things that adults look for when they're thinking of going back to the classroom. As you go down the list, look at each item in terms of its relative importance to you. The *"musts"* are things that are absolutely critical in making it possible to go back to school; the *"wants"* are desirable and will certainly make it easier; the *"don't cares"* aren't important to you. For example, if you are a single parent with no friends or family living nearby who can help take care of your child and no means of paying a baby sitter, then a campus child-care center is a must. If you already have a good baby sitter but think it would be more convenient to have your child in a nursery school on campus, that would be a want. But if you have no children, or if your child has an older sibling who can always baby sit, or if your children are grown and gone, then you probably don't care whether there is a child-care center on campus.

In exercise 4-1, some possible wants and needs are suggested, but don't limit yourself to these items. Add your own list of expectations and then check off the appropriate column.

▼ **Exercise 4-1:** Musts and Wants

Item	Must Have	Want/ Prefer	Doesn't Matter
A special program in _____ (fill in).			
A strong department of _____.			
A college within _____ miles of home or work.			
Late afternoon or evening child care service.			
Bus or train service to campus.			
Free parking on campus.			
All required courses offered after 5 p.m.			
School Calendar: flexible? convenient? realistic?			
Availability of independent study, telecourses, etc.			
Library open on Sundays			

Item	Must Have	Want/ Prefer	Doesn't Matter
Prior Learning Assessment program available.			
CLEP exams?			
ACE evaluation of military and corporate courses?			
Portfolio assessment?			
Others (fill in your own specific needs)			

Keep your musts and wants in mind as you go through the following material, remembering always that even the "best" schools are good for you only if they offer what you need.

▲

▲ How Schools and Colleges Work

If you wish to become a smart consumer of higher education, you should be able to "speak college;" that is, you should understand terms such as *semester* and *credit hour,* know the difference between degree and non-degree study, and, in general, be able to make decisions about your own schooling based on a solid understanding of what is and is not available, possible, or desirable for you. (For quick reference to the meaning of unfamiliar terms used here or elsewhere, see the glossary.)

There are many kinds of postsecondary (after high school) schools and colleges in the United States which fulfill different needs. Some of these are listed below.

Two-year or community colleges. These are closely related to the communities supporting them. They offer associate of arts (A.A.), associate of science (A.S.) or associate of applied science (A.A.S.) degrees as well as non-credit courses covering a large range of vocational, technical and academic subjects. Most community colleges have a high percentage of part-time adult students and offer many of their classes and services at hours convenient to working people.

Community colleges usually have arrangements for transferring credits earned there to four-year colleges, but special conditions sometimes apply to certificate or A.A.S. programs. Students should check on these special conditions prior to beginning programs from which they hope to transfer credit.

Because they are state and locally supported, community colleges are usually less expensive than other colleges.

Colleges. These offer bachelor's degrees (four years of full-time study, considerably more to complete a degree on a part-time basis) in liberal arts and sciences as well as in some vocational/professional areas. Most colleges also offer some continuing education, and adult weekend or evening courses and programs. Colleges differ widely in their percentage of residential and non-residential students, in their emphasis on the purely academic versus vocational/technical subjects, and in their desire to attract and serve adults.

Universities. These are usually made up of a collection of graduate and professional schools that offer master's degrees and doctorates, and an undergraduate division that awards bachelor's degrees. In general, their admissions standards tend to be higher, and most put emphasis on research as well as teaching.

To accommodate their adult students, most universities have evening and/or weekend classes as well as a non-credit continuing education division.

Proprietary schools. These are privately owned, for-profit schools that usually focus on one or more technological or vocational areas, such as electronics, computers, paralegal studies. In most states they must be licensed, and in some states they are permitted to award degrees as well as certificates. However, caution should be exercised regarding the transferability of their credits to other institutions.

Adult community-based schools. These are typically sponsored by local school districts, churches, labor unions, YMCAs, women's groups, and other community organizations. Their courses typically cover a wide range of subjects and are designed to serve the needs of the sponsoring organization's constituencies. The courses are of varying length and intellectual depth. They tend to focus on practical and cultural subjects or on current issues. They do not carry credit.

Vocational/Technical schools. These may be sponsored by a state or local community, and may have transfer arrangements with the local high schools or community colleges. They train people for specific trades or occupations.

As you can see, there is a wide variety of schools, each serving somewhat different needs and constituencies. If you want to get a two-year degree in a technical area such as automotive technology or commercial art, then you will want to look closely at your local community college to see if it offers the desired program. And if you want eventually to teach junior high school science, then you will look to a four-year college that offers degrees in education, or a university that offers the possibility of going on to graduate study. But if you want to learn a trade such as electronics or a practical skill such as welding, you will probably want to investigate your local community college, vo-tech schools, and proprietary schools to compare their programs and determine how long the course of study is, what it costs, and how much help each institution will give you in finding a job.

Joan B.'s (see profile, chapter 2, p. 15) search for an appropriate school is a case in point. Joan's immediate goal is to get a bachelor of arts degree in art history, with the eventual goal of going on to a graduate school of business. The university in her midwestern city has both a bachelor's program in art history, and a graduate program in business, but its tuition is rather expensive. Initially, she thought she might save some money by taking the first two years of college at her local community college, where she could also have her considerable learnings in art assessed for prior learning credit. She hoped then to transfer to the university to complete her bachelor's degree and go on to work on her master's. However, after making some phone calls to registrars of the two schools, she learned that the university in her city does not accept assessment credits in transfer, nor will it accept any credits in the student's "major" that were earned at a community college. If she wants to use her prior learning toward her degree, she will have to register initially at the university and have her learning assessed there. By taking the initiative to do the research before she registered, Joan has saved herself a lot of frustration and duplication of effort.

▲ Independent Learning

Going back to college, even obtaining a college degree, doesn't necessarily mean that you have to attend classes in the traditional way for a certain number of hours per week. Perhaps you live in a rural area, quite far from the nearest school and without access to

Participating in an independent program requires the ability to study and learn on your own. You will be setting your own study hours and exercising self-discipline in completing your assignments.

transportation. Perhaps you have two toddlers and no one with whom to leave them. Or your work may call for a tremendous amount of travel, which makes it unlikely that you could get to class regularly. Or you may be housebound by illness or a handicapping condition. Or you may simply prefer independent to class study. In any case, there are a number of ways in which you can get a college education without taking all your courses and earning all your credit sitting in a traditional classroom.

Several well known "independent learning" colleges (see appendix D for a partial list with addresses and phone numbers) make programs available to adult learners for whom traditional classroom study may be difficult or impossible. These colleges have developed ways of working with students at a distance through phones, faxes, programmed materials, computer courses, regular or e-mail, interactive TV, and all sorts of mechanisms which enable individuals to study alone but under the supervision of concerned faculty and within the jurisdiction of accredited college programs.

All of these institutions are committed to finding ways to support the student who rarely, if ever, can attend a class or meet face-to-face with a professor. Each has graduated hundreds of adults whose degrees have opened up for them avenues of personal and professional advancement. Some of them offer assessment of prior learning, and all of them accommodate part-time study.

Other, more traditional colleges and universities frequently offer a diversity of options, including independent study, study at extension divisions, credit for correspondence, or television courses and other comparable ways of learning. Check this out at your local college.

Participating in an independent learning program requires a strong commitment to learning and the ability to learn on your own. It means that you will have to reschedule your life to find regular time for study and enlist the understanding of other members of your household. It may mean making use of local learning resources such as libraries, television programs, museums, workplaces, churches, videos, computers. At some schools it may mean working with faculty to design your own learning contracts—that is, deciding what you intend to study, what learning resources you will use, what activities you will carry out, and what criteria will be used to evaluate your progress. In other schools you may be working on courses with pre-set written, taped, or computer materials. You may be communicating with the professor through phone, fax, modem, regular or e-mail. You will be setting your own study hours and exercising self-discipline in completing your assignments, keeping in touch with the professor or mentor, and persevering toward completion and success.

Many independent learners miss the opportunity to exchange ideas with their teachers and other students in a face-to-face situation, to discuss, to argue, to get different points of view. Recognizing the importance of such interchange, some of the colleges that offer independent learning options have set up weekend seminars or two-week summer workshops at which independent learners can meet on topics of common interest and learn together.

The colleges that offer independent learning have given thousands of adult students the freedom to work from their own homes, at their own pace, and on their own schedule. On farms, in small towns, in nursing homes, in large cities, even in prisons, people who might otherwise have had to give up their dreams of a college education are currently participating in independent learning opportunities.

▲ Learning to "Speak College"

An important determinant of your choice of schools is whether what you need is simply a few courses, credit or non-credit, a certificate, or a degree. The next thing you want to understand is the meaning of these terms.

Non-credit courses. These are offered by a variety of institutions to fulfill the needs of people for instruction in the arts and sciences, professional fields, self-help (such as time management and holistic healing), personal enrichment (poetry writing, wine tasting, stenciling) and vocational skills. There are no rules about how long these courses should be or who should be permitted to teach them. However, the non-credit offerings at some institutions are among the most innovative learning opportunities in the country.

Credit courses. These are offered by accredited colleges and universities and typically take about 12–15 hours of classroom time per credit (with equal or double that expected in reading and research outside the classroom). A credit course may be part of a degree or certificate program or may simply be taken as a single entity. It may take place over the period of a semester, a month, or a single intensive weekend.

Continuing education units (CEUs). CEUs are nontraditional "credit" carried by some continuing education courses, designed to meet the requirements of specific professional organizations in areas such as nursing, law, medicine, social work, accounting, engineering, etc. Since CEUs are awarded on the basis of attendance rather than of learning acquired, most schools do not attempt to equate them with college credit.

Certificate programs. These are designed to cover a specific field such as management information systems, paralegal studies, or auto body repair. They may consist of anywhere from two to twelve courses, and may be open in some cases to people with no previous college experience. In other cases a college degree or certain relevant courses may be prerequisites. In some situations a certificate can be earned on the way to getting a degree, and the credits earned will apply to that degree. (If you want to keep all options open, you will want to check this out prior to beginning a certificate program.)

Associate's degrees. These include the associate of arts (A.A.), the associate of science (A.S.), the associate of applied science (A.A.S.), the associate of professional studies (A.P.S.) and a number of variations. The associate's is typically a two-year degree[1] requiring about 60 credits. (Part-time study may increase the time to four to six years.) In some, but not all, cases the credits can be transferred to a four-year college.

Bachelor's degrees. These include the bachelor of arts (B.A.), the bachelor of science (B.S.), the bachelor of professional studies (B.P.S.) and numerous variations. The bachelor's degree usually requires about 120 credits (four years of full-time study).

Master's degrees. These include the master of arts (M.A.), the master of science (M.S.), master of library science (M.L.S.), master of social work (M.S.W), etc. They are typically 30 to 36 credit programs (beyond the bachelor's degree) and may require a research project culminating in the writing of a thesis. Some master's programs include a substantial amount of field work and may require up to 60 credits.

---

[1] In the description of this and other degrees, the average time stated is for full-time study, which generally means taking from 12 to 15 credits per semester. Since most adult students cannot study full-time, the length of time needed to complete the degree may be double or more.

Doctoral degrees. These include the doctor of philosophy (Ph.D.), the doctor of laws (LL.D. or J.D.), the doctor of medicine (M.D.), the doctor of education (Ed.D.), etc. They usually require about 60 hours of graduate study, and most require completion of a major research study or dissertation.

▲ Credit versus Non-Credit Study

Don't let all of this discussion of degrees make you think that learning is only worthwhile if you get a piece of paper saying you have earned a few initials. Not everyone wants or needs to study towards a degree. Indeed there are **advantages to non-degree study:**

You can learn what you want or need to learn without having to take specific courses to fulfill degree requirements.

You can go at your own pace, in credit or non-credit courses.

You can concentrate less on grades and more on what you are learning for its own sake.

And, of course there are also **advantages to degrees or certificates:**

Degrees and certificates are passports to some jobs in real estate, teaching, business management, etc.

They are necessary for some licensed professions, such as engineering, nursing, dentistry, accounting, etc.

A degree or certificate signifies to the world and yourself that you have acquired a significant amount of learning in a particular field.

A degree is more easily transferable than a collection of courses if you wish to go on for a higher degree.

You have something to hang on the wall that people recognize.

▲ Getting the Information You Need

A while back we compared choosing a school to choosing a new car or washing machine or place to vacation. You have probably come to the conclusion that choosing a school makes the other decisions look easy, and you may be getting nervous about how to find out all of the things you want to know.

Well, it's not really that difficult. If you were choosing a place to vacation, you would probably begin by deciding what the high priority items were for you and your family (musts and wants). Let's say you wanted to go where it was warm, near the water so your children could swim and you could fish, near a golf course, and relatively inexpensive.

You might begin by talking to friends who had recently gone away. Let's say a few of them recommended Florida, but disagreed on whether you should go to the east or west coast, or whether you should stay at a beach hotel, a motel on the bay or a resort near Disney World.

You might then read an article in a travel magazine which would give you more specific information on Florida, and you would probably want to talk to a travel agent to find out about the various resorts available.

Your next step would probably be to look over some brochures that you received from the travel agent or that you had written away for. You would compare locations, facilities, prices, and general attractiveness. As in all decisions, you would have to set some priorities: should you pay more to stay in a hotel with a great restaurant, or is it better to have your own kitchen? Would you rather be right on the beach, a block away where the rent is lower, or back in the town? Should you pass up a terrific bargain in Miami Beach to be closer to friends who live in Tampa?

Finding out about schools is not as different from this process—or as difficult—as you may think. You have a similar range of resources for information:

▲ friends and relatives who have gone back to school
▲ college admissions officers, counselors, and professors
▲ the guidance counselor at your local high school
▲ the human resources or training specialist at your place of employment
▲ public information sessions that are given at many colleges
▲ printed materials
    college catalogs and brochures (available in libraries and your local high school, but you can also order them by phone directly from the colleges)

▲ standard college guides like Barron's or Peterson's (available in libraries)

▲ ads and articles in the education section of your newspaper

▲ Using College Catalogs

The college catalog is the primary way in which a school communicates with prospective students. It contains a wealth of information about the mission of the institution, its status with state and national accrediting agencies, its range of degrees and programs, its educational philosophy, and the degrees and attainments of its faculty. It also has detailed information about such practical matters as admissions policies, tuition charges, degrees offered, course and credit requirements, the school calendar, grading, special programs and the like.

The catalog is also a public relations tool, however. It is carefully designed to present the image the school wishes to convey. A careful reading of the catalog, including a close look at the illustrations, will tell you a great deal about the institution that will be valuable to you in making your choice, but you will probably have to discover many things, both positive and negative, for yourself. Don't forget your musts and wants.

If you can find answers to the list of questions in exercise 4-2, you'll have a good general sense of what you can expect from a college and what it will expect from you. An up close, properly skeptical look at the catalog of the school you plan to attend will answer most of these questions as well as others you may have.

▼ **Exercise 4-2:** Important Questions to Ask About Colleges

1. What are the admissions criteria for adults in this school?

2. Is there any special reference to adult or "nontraditional" students under admissions policies?

3. Are there any prerequisites (courses you should already have completed) for the course/program you are planning to take?

4. What department gives the course/program you want? (If it is a non-credit course, it may be in the continuing education bulletin and not in this catalog.)

5. How long will it take you to complete the program or degree? To figure this out you will have to know:

   ▲ the total number of courses in the program/degree

   ▲ the number of courses you may have already completed through an earlier time in college, through evaluated course work in a military or corporate setting, or through being assessed for learning you have accomplished on your own.

   ▲ how many courses you expect to take per semester or per year

6. Is there a program of **prior learning assessment** or admission with advanced standing? (See exercise 4-3 for a list of more specific questions you should ask about prior learning assessment.)

7. Is any mention made of whether degrees can be completed on a part-time basis or does the school require full-time status?

8. Are adult students or working students mentioned (or pictured) at all? How often?

9. Is it clear from the catalog whether one can complete a degree by taking courses in the late afternoon, evenings or weekends?

10. How much time do you have at the beginning of a semester to withdraw from a course without penalty?

11. Does the school have the following services available for adult students:

    ▲ child care (late afternoons and evenings)?

    ▲ career counseling?

    ▲ academic advising?

    ▲ financial aid?

    ▲ basic skills workshops or tutoring?

12. Do adult students have to fulfill requirements that are more appropriate to younger students, such as physical education, payment of student activity or health fees, etc.?

13. What fees does the school charge in addition to tuition?

14. Are there many pictures in the catalog of older people or minorities?

15. What kind of clothes are the students wearing? Are they dressed up or casual?

16. Do the pictures of classrooms show large lecture sections or smaller, more intimate groups?

▲

Once you have acquired this general information and have determined that you want your knowledge assessed for college credit, you will also need some information on the institution's views of, and procedures for, the assignment of credit for prior learning. Exercise 4-3 poses some questions on this issue for which you will want answers.

▼ **Exercise 4-3:** What You Need to Find Out About Assessment

If you've already determined that you want to have your skills and knowledge assessed for college credit, you will need to get answers to the following questions:

1. Does the institution you plan to attend give credit or recognition for learning acquired outside a formal school setting?

2. Does it offer some or all of the following alternatives?

   ▲ Portfolio assessment

   ▲ Credit by examination (CLEP, ACT-PEP, DANTES, etc.)

   ▲ Challenge exams

   ▲ Acceptance of ACE recommendations on noncollegiate sponsored instruction (PONSI)

   ▲ Acceptance of ACE recommendations on military education

   ▲ Other

3. Does the institution have a limit on the number of credits you can earn by way of these methods? (At some institutions, separate limits are set on credits earned by each means—credit by examination, correspondence, PONSI, ACE military, or portfolio. At others they are lumped together. Make sure you find out your institution's policy before you begin. You want to be sure that the options offered will work to your advantage.)

4. Can credits earned through assessment apply to any aspect of your degree program or only to a selected portion: to your major, for example, or only to free electives?

5. Will credits awarded for your prior learning, through any of the means offered above, be applied to your degree program immediately or only after particular course requirements have been met?

6. When can you begin the assessment process:
   ▲ before you register at the college?
   ▲ during the first semester?
   ▲ after you have met certain requirements?
   ▲ anytime?

7. What printed materials, guidelines, and forms are provided for you to use?

8. If you have chosen to do portfolio-assisted assessment, what personal assistance does the institution provide, such as workshops, advisors, or a course on assessment?

9. Is there a restriction on the length of time in which you must complete your portfolio or other forms of assessment?

10. If you choose to do a portfolio, who will assess it after it is developed:
    ▲ college faculty?
    ▲ assessment office personnel?
    ▲ experts external to the institution?

11. How and by whom are credit recommendations made?

12. Can you appeal a credit recommendation decision if it does not seem fair? If so, how?

13. What are the fees? Is there a blanket charge for assessment, or will you be charged by the credit? If the latter, is it based on the credits requested or the credit granted? And what is the correlation between the fees for assessment and the regular course fees?

14. How much time will the assessment process take? Is the time and cost to your benefit?

15. Does the school's assessment program conform to CAEL's "Ten Standards for Quality Assurance in Assessing Learning for Credit" (see appendix A)?

▲

Many of these questions may seem a bit overwhelming, but it is important that you get the answers before you register, not after. More than likely, your institution will have a well staffed prior learning assessment office, an adult learning service office, a testing and assessment office, a continuing education department, or an external degree programs office, with counselors or advisors who can give you the answers you need. Sample tests and preparation booklets for CLEP and other exams should be available. If you are interested in a portfolio assessment option, they may also have samples of other students' portfolios for you to review.

Don't be afraid to ask other questions you may think of, no matter how unimportant they may seem. Undertaking the assessment process requires a strong commitment of time, effort, and money. You want to be sure that you know as clearly as possible what will be expected of you so that you can put your best effort toward demonstrating that you really do possess the college-level knowledge or competency you claim to have.

▲ Follow-Up Activities

Some kinds of information about how a school "feels" are not readily available, either from people or printed information. To get a real sense of a school, you should probably take yourself on a campus tour, talking to students as well as to school officials, looking over the library, the bookstore, the cafeterias or student "hangouts," perhaps even sitting in on a class or two. Most professors will welcome you if you arrange for such a visit ahead of time.

A personal visit is a great way to find out how long it takes to drive to the campus, how crowded the parking lot is, how the dining hall hamburgers taste, and how many students are in your age group. Use the guide in chapter 8, pp. 133–134, to help organize your tour.

▲ Hedging Your Bets

It is important to recognize that what you want today may change, and the decisions you make now about schools, programs, and courses may also have to change. At any point in your life, the choices you make are conditioned by habits of mind, events, and temporary circumstances that can alter. Don't worry too much about possibly making the "wrong" decisions. Many adults have found that returning to school profoundly changes their sense of what they want to accomplish, what they want to study, and how they choose to study it. If, despite serious thinking about it, you're still not sure exactly what you want to do, you're in good company. One of the exciting things about education is that it gets people thinking more explicitly about where they're heading in life and why.

Even if you change your mind after six months in school, your early decisions won't be "mistakes" if, as a smart consumer, you have hedged your bets.

Some useful strategies for hedging your bets include:

▲ Start with one or two basic courses that will be useful in a number of different programs. For instance, courses in English are usually required or recommended in any program.

▲ Take a basic course in your own specialty to see how you like it and how well you do. If Dorene (see profiles, chapter 2, p. 15) was still uncertain about whether she wanted to work toward a degree in computer science or take a certificate program in management information systems (MIS), she could take a course in computer programming that is a requirement in both.

▲ Make certain the courses you take in College A will be easily transferable to Colleges B and C. This enables you to keep open your option to switch schools if your first choice doesn't work out. Introductory courses in basic subjects such as English and mathematics are usually easier to transfer than unusual or specialized courses.

▲ A Note of Caution

While finding out about the availability of PLA in the school you plan to attend, it would also be wise to check the institution's practices, its means of assessing learning, against the standards for quality assurance in appendix A. First, you want to make certain that mechanisms are in place to assure you a fair, reliable, unbiased assessment and that there are provisions for appeal. Second, you want to be wary of too "easy" an assessment process. If you are offered credit for your "experience" without reference to what you've learned from that experience, be suspicious. You may be dealing with an institution whose PLA practices are open to question. While the prospect of "easy" credit is seductive, in the long run it may make those credits less transferable to other institutions and thus less valuable.

You may wish to return to this chapter more than once as you become involved in the actual process of returning to school, but for now let's turn our attention to the major issue in this book: how to get college credit for learning you have accomplished on your own.

5

Prior Learning Assessment: Getting Credit for What You Know

And long experience made him sage.

John Gay

In the previous chapter's discussion on how to choose a college, it was suggested that one of your criteria might be whether or not the school had a program of prior learning assessment. **Prior learning assessment (PLA) is a process whereby any learning you have acquired before the assessment and have not had transcripted by a college is evaluated to determine whether it is comparable with what is taught in college, and, if so, is recognized by the award of college credit.**

In this and the following chapters, we will be looking at all aspects of PLA: why it's useful to adult students, how it works, and what you can do right now to get started on the path to getting credit for what you have learned.

But first, if you are like most adults, you're probably wondering whether you have any learning that is "assessable." You may even have doubts that you still have the ability to learn. These are legitimate questions that deserve serious thought.

▲ The Adult as an Accomplished Learner

The typical adult's worries about loss of learning abilities are usually groundless. Let us deal first with your doubts about your ability to learn. If you have any teenagers at home, you might compare yourself with them. They may be quicker to memorize facts or to solve mathematical puzzles than you, but do they have your ability to call upon past knowledge or experience when confronting a problem, communicating, or using critical reasoning? Do they have the vast number of specific skills you have accumulated that will make learning new ones easier? Do they have as clear a sense of purpose or as strong a commitment to what they are doing?

Adults' experience and maturity give them an advantage over their younger classmates. As students, they typically have a better sense of what they want to learn and why, and in order to go back to school, they have made sacrifices in time, money, and life style that bolster their determination to succeed. As a result, most studies show that adult students do very well in the classroom, typically meeting or exceeding the performance of traditional college age students.

▲ You as a Learner

You are already an accomplished learner. You've been learning all your life.

Just think about the learning you demonstrate just to get through each day. Think about your domestic learning: about how you shop, plan, and cook meals, make household repairs, attend to car maintenance, care for children. Or about your work learning: how you function in a factory or office or hospital or store or on the streets of the city. What an enormous number of things you have to know and be able to do to function successfully. Or think about your non-work-related learning: what do you have to know to prepare the soil for your vegetable garden, or carry on a discussion about the drug problem, or lead your church choir, or refinish your best friend's antique cupboard?

To begin to focus on your prior learning, complete exercise 5-1.

▼ **Exercise 5-1:** Focusing on a Learning Experience

Think of an important learning experience you've had in the last six months. It might have been on the job, at home, or in your community. You may have learned how to use a computer, set up a tropical fish tank, or conduct a mail campaign for the local Policemen's Benevolent Society. Don't worry right now about whether this learning is college level. If you took the time to learn it, it must have been important to you, and it demonstrates your ability as a learner.

Take a few minutes to make some notes about this learning experience:

What did you learn?

How did you learn it?

Where did you learn it?

Why did you learn it?

▲

The *what* of learning is important for a prior learning assessment program. If you can say "I learned to create and use a spreadsheet program on the computer," or "I learned to dismantle and repair my VCR," or "I learned why taking an accurate census is politically crucial to my party," you will have taken the first step toward recognizing your own learning. This sounds obvious, but the problem many people have in undertaking prior learning assessment is in being specific about naming or defining their own learning. They will say something like, "Well, I know a lot about construction or social work or transportation," but they have difficulty in narrowing down these terms to exactly what it is they actually know or can do.

The *how* of learning leads you to recognize the various ways in which adults learn and helps you begin to understand your own learning style. People learn from watching and listening to experts, from reading, from doing and experimenting, and by comparing past experience with new experience (reflecting).

The *where* of learning should suggest to you the almost endless number of sources of learning in the modern world. We may learn from:

formal instruction (in school, on the job, in the military, in classes sponsored by churches and community organizations);

working—on the job experiential learning (trying things out, experimenting, watching fellow workers);

reading books, articles, newspapers, directions;

radio, television, videos, CDs;

observation of other people;

questioning of friends, relatives, co-workers, supervisors, experts;

computer programs, Internet, and traveling.

Perhaps most profound of all is the *why* of learning. We learn because we need some information or we need to know how to do something. The *why* of learning is critical because if we don't have a reason, we won't learn. Some of the reasons people give for learning are:

to keep up with technological change in the workplace

to prepare for a new career

to help get through a difficult life transition, such as divorce, a family death, kids growing up and moving away

to improve their ability to participate in community affairs or do volunteer work on a more professional basis

to meet new people and make new friends

to become more proficient in a sport or hobby

to "keep up" with friends or family members

to get a degree or license or certificate

to prepare for retirement

to get a GED (the equivalent of a high school degree)

to improve their communication skills

to achieve the satisfaction of learning something new

All learning is valuable. If you have taken the time to learn something, it's probably because that learning was going to be useful to you in some way. You should value your learnings and take pride in yourself as a learner, whether or not the things you have learned are similar to what is taught in college.

But if you are contemplating returning to college in the near future, or if you have sometimes wished you could go to college without repeating courses in what you already know, you should seriously consider the possibility of **assessment of your prior learning for college credit.**

▲ The Background of PLA Programs

Assessment of prior learning is not a new idea. Some colleges have for many years had "advanced placement" programs in which they routinely tested incoming freshman for English or foreign language or mathematics skills, placing them in advanced courses in those subjects if they did well. Some professors informally counsel students who are already highly proficient in the materials of an introductory course—computer science, for instance, or basic office procedures—to skip that course and take more advanced classes.

But the practice of assessing prior learning as a systematic way of finding out what college level skills and knowledge adult students bring with them and evaluating those skills and knowledge for college credit, is now more than fifty years old. It may be said to have begun right after World War II, when the American Council on Education (ACE) began offering recommendations for college credit awards for learning in the military services. Formalized testing programs as a means of assessing prior learning made their appearance in the mid-sixties. The assessment movement, however, can be said to have begun in 1974 with an organization called the Council for Adult and Experiential Learning (CAEL). CAEL was interested in the extent and variety of learnings that people acquire on their own and was dedicated to researching methods that would enable educational institutions to do *valid, reliable* assessment of learning acquired outside those institutions.

Since 1974, one of CAEL's major purposes has been to research and promote the formal assessment and recognition of college-level learning of two kinds not commonly recognized by credit or advancement in standing: 1) that acquired before the assessment by the current institution and not previously transcripted; and 2) that acquired under the sponsorship of the current institution via practice, internships, apprenticeships, and other hands-on experiences occurring off campus. Today CAEL is active in helping colleges and universities set up programs to examine and evaluate individuals' formal and experiential learnings,[1] and, when they are found equivalent to what is taught in college, grant credit for them. It also has a quality assurance program to monitor and evaluate current assessment programs (see appendix A).

A number of fine colleges and universities in the United States (and Canada, Great Britain, New Zealand, and Australia) have recognized that what adults learn on their own or through their work can be quite similar to what is taught in the classroom. These schools have set up programs to identify, evaluate, and award credit for college-level learning, no matter where or how it was acquired. (See appendix J for an annotated list of such institutions in the U.S.)

▲ Why PLA Programs are Important

You may wonder why assessment of prior learning is considered so important. Well, simple fairness is one reason. Suppose Kate, an office worker responsible for keeping the financial records of a small manufacturing company, has taught herself the principles of accounting by working out a functional bookkeeping system, attending company-based training workshops, reading accounting textbooks, and putting theory into practice. Why shouldn't she get the same credit for what she knows as a person who takes Accounting 101 at a local community college?

Or suppose Bill, who has been running a support program for AIDS victims through his church and has learned group counsel-

---

[1] Experiential learning is any learning in which the learner is in direct touch with the realities being studied. In other words, it is learning by doing, by hands-on practice. For example, learning management by taking a company-sponsored training class is formal or non-experiential. Learning management by trial and error as you deal with five persons who work under your supervision is experiential. A combination of non-experiential learning, which emphasizes theory, and experiential learning, which emphasizes practice, can lead to a richer education than either of these alone.

ing techniques from the social workers and minister involved in the program, wants to go back to school to get a degree in social work. Why shouldn't the university to which he has applied evaluate what he has already learned about counseling to see how closely it approximates what is taught in the school's own counseling courses?

Beyond the issue of simple fairness, prior learning assessment (PLA) programs mean tremendous savings of time and money. Busy adults who go back to school have to juggle the time spent in class and study along with the demands of jobs and families and community responsibilities. Their time is limited and very valuable to them. If by earning one or two semester's worth of credit through PLA they can shorten the length of time necessary to achieve a degree, the pressures on them will be considerably lighter.

Similarly, most adults returning to school are making a considerable financial sacrifice, paying for tuition, books and supplies, transportation, possibly for baby sitters. If the number of courses they must take is lessened by PLA, the savings can be significant.

Even those adults whose employer is paying for their education through tuition reimbursement or pre-paid tuition, can benefit financially from PLA. Most tuition plans have a cap or ceiling on the total amount that can be spent on education. If some courses can be recognized through PLA, there may be more funding available for more advanced courses.

PLA is also useful in defining what students *don't* know, which can be very helpful in planning their courses of study. For example, in her job with an international bank, Judy had acquired considerable learning in management and finance but had no opportunity to learn much about marketing or customer relations. In going through the PLA process, she not only validated her own strengths in management and finance, she also discovered the limits of her learning and decided to include marketing, consumer psychology, and customer relations in her degree program. Jules, who has been working as a designer's assistant for seven years and hopes to earn a degree in industrial design, found out through the assessment process that his experience with computer-aided design (CAD) is too superficial to qualify for college credit. He is planning to take courses in CAD to address this deficiency.

Finally, and perhaps most important it is gratifying to achieve recognition for learning that you have accomplished on your own. Most people who have gone through the process of prior learning assessment report that, as they began to realize the extent and quality of their learning, they gained in confidence and self-esteem.

Today, as more and more adults are going back to the classroom, and as the average age of community college students in the United States has risen to 37 years, hundreds of colleges and universities have recognized the wealth of learning that these adult students bring with them, and have responded by offering testing options and/or creating prior learning assessment programs. These programs have enabled thousands of adult learners like yourself to gain recognition and credit for the college-level learning they have accomplished on their own.

If you consult appendix J for the list of institutions offering PLA, you will probably find one or more in your geographic area. Then, if after finishing this book you think you may qualify for college credit for what you have learned, you will know where to start your search for the school that is right for you.

CHAPTER

6

Some Methods Institutions Use to Evaluate Your Prior Learning

Nothing in education is so astonishing as the amount of ignorance it accumulates in the form of inert facts.

Henry Brooks Adams

By now you should be convinced that you have indeed acquired considerable learning over your lifetime and that some of that learning may be the equivalent of what you could have learned in a college. Let's review some of the methods used to translate learning from life experience into college credits.

transfer of transcript credit

articulation agreements among colleges and other institutions

proficiency examinations

credit for the completion of evaluated programs: military, corporate or union

credit for previously evaluated licenses, certificates, apprenticeships, etc.

credit by portfolio-assisted assessment

In the following pages we will look closely at the first five of these
options. Then, in chapter 7, we will go on to an in-depth explanation of portfolio-assisted assessment, including detailed instructions
for developing and assembling a portfolio.

If the number of areas in which you hope to earn credit are limited to learning that derives from a source that can either be documented by a transcript, or evaluated by an examination, or is con-
tained in a previously evaluated program, you may not have to
produce a portfolio. If your learnings are less "neat," however, that
is, if you do not have transcripts, can't locate standardized exams
that cover the knowledge you think you have gained, and haven't
been involved in programs that have been evaluated, you will probably want to consider the development of a portfolio. If this is the
case, you will need to choose a school which offers a portfolio assessment program (see appendix J).

▲ College Transcripts

A college transcript is an official record of courses taken, grades
earned, credit received, and degrees granted. If you attended a college at some time in the past, even if it was 20 or 30 years ago, that
college still has all the necessary information about you on file, and
some or all of the credit earned may transfer to the institution at
which you have chosen to complete your degree. You can obtain a
copy of your academic record by writing to the registrar of each
school you attended, requesting a transcript. You will need to provide the dates of your attendance and the name or names under
which you were registered. (Women who changed their names upon
marriage sometimes forget to inform the school of the change, and
then wonder why their records seem to be missing.) There is usually a fee of a few dollars for each transcript you request. You can
find out the amount of the fee and any other regulations the school
may have by calling the registrar's office. Be sure that you sign your
request because the registrar will need your authorization in order
to release the record.

You can use copies of your old transcripts for your own information, or to work on while you are going through the assessment process, but schools will ask for official transcripts when they are asked to accept them as documentation for transfer credit. An official transcript is one which bears the original imprint of the college seal. Usually it must be mailed directly from one college to the other, though some schools will accept an original that is hand delivered by the student, as long as the imprint is clear.

Do not be discouraged if your old transcripts contain some mediocre or low grades. Registrars know that most people tend to do much better when they return to school as adults than they did when they were younger. Your grades, as long as they are "C's" or better, will probably not have much weight in whether or not your credits can be transferred. If you failed courses earlier in your college career, those credits will not transfer, but the presence of several failing grades should not deter you from presenting the transcript.

However, some colleges have rules about how "old" the credits are. That is, they may have regulations that prevent the acceptance of credits that you earned too far in the past. This is particularly true in fields in the sciences and technologies, which are constantly changing, and in which what you learned 14 years ago may by now have been superseded by new research findings. Some schools also have rules about the total maximum number of credits they will accept. They may restrict credit transfer to subjects other than your "major," or they may accept only those courses that are similar to those in their own catalogs. Since schools differ widely in their practices in this regard, questions regarding transferability should become part of your own college interview process.

Don't let these rules discourage you from trying to use as much of your previous credit as you can. If you can make a logical argument for the credit's currency and validity in your degree program (without being rude or combative), you may be able to persuade the officials that it would be fair to make an exception in your case. More than one "rule" has been suspended to accommodate adult students who present a logical case for the validity of using the credit they earned somewhere else.

▲ Articulation Agreements

Some colleges have agreements among themselves that they will accept each other's transcripted credits, including degrees awarded, without questioning individual courses. This is particularly true within geographic regions where there is a close relationship between the community college and the four year college, and where each institution respects the other's academic programs. Other kinds of articulation agreements may exist between a college and a proprietary school with a particularly strong program that the college does not offer, or between a college and a local corporation that offers quality employee training. In these cases, the student's task in making the case for getting credit for the learnings is made considerably easier. Officials in the assessment office of your school will be able to tell you if any articulation agreement exists that will impact on the learnings you plan to present.

▲ Credit by Examination

A number of different examination programs have been created to evaluate learning that has been acquired outside the classroom. One or more of the following kinds of exams may provide a good fit with your learning, in which case taking an exam may prove to be the least complicated way for you to earn credit.[1] (See appendix E for further information on testing organizations.)

1. *CLEP* (College Level Examination Program) is probably the most widely used method of testing learning that adults have acquired outside the classroom. It is available at testing centers across the country, including most large public libraries and many community colleges. Where you take the exam is not important; what does matter is the policy of your selected school regarding the award of credit on the basis of performance in CLEP exams.

   There are two kinds of CLEP exams—general and subject exams.

---

[1] In addition to the standard examination programs listed below, there are several others that are sponsored by colleges such as Ohio University, Regents College of the University of the State of New York, and Thomas A. Edison State College in New Jersey. You can find out more about these programs by writing to the sponsoring organization at the addresses provided in appendix D.

▲ *General.* Each of the general exams covers material taught in courses that most students take as requirements in the first two years of college. Each is 90 minutes long, and except for the English Composition version with essay,[2] each consists entirely of multiple choice questions to be answered in two separately timed sections. From three to six semester hours of credit are usually awarded for satisfactory scores on each general examination. General examinations are given in the following areas: English composition, humanities, mathematics, social sciences and history, and natural sciences.

The general exams are useful if you have broad knowledge in one of these fields equivalent to what you would have learned in the first two years of college.

You can choose to take all of the general exams or only those with which you feel comfortable. You will not be penalized for doing poorly in the exams, but if your scores meet the college's expectations, you can accumulate a substantial amount of college credit. Be sure to check with the institution you have chosen regarding its policy on CLEP general exams.

▲ *Subject.* Each subject examination covers material taught in an undergraduate course with a similar title at most colleges and universities. A college that accepts CLEP subject exams usually grants the same amount of credit to students earning satisfactory scores as it grants to students passing that course.

2. *ACT-PEP Regents College Examinations.* The ACT-PEP exams cover 42 courses, including education, arts and sciences, business, and nursing.

3. *DANTES Subject Standardized Tests* (DSSTs). Originally designed for and available only to military personnel, these tests may now be taken by the civilian population as well. Over 30 tests cover such subject areas as physical science, social science, business, applied technology, humanities and mathematics.

---

[2] Many schools require that you take the English exam with essay. Check this out before you register for the exam.

4. *Job Ready Level Assessment Tests.* This testing program is particularly useful for assessing the competency of students with learning in a broad range of vocational and technical fields.

5. *Advanced Placement Program* (AP). Intended primarily for high school students, these examinations may be taken by anyone, regardless of age or background. They are in primarily academic subjects such as English, history, chemistry, and mathematics.

6. *GRE.* Graduate Record Examinations, ordinarily taken as a prerequisite for admission to graduate school, are occasionally used for assessment of prior learning at the undergraduate level.

7. *Challenge Examinations.* These are exams designed by the school, the department, or the faculty member responsible for the course that corresponds to the area of learning for which you are requesting credit. In other words, if you think that your learning in human anatomy is equivalent to what is being taught in a course in human anatomy, some schools will invite you to take a challenge exam in that subject.

    Up to this point, all of the exams discussed have been standardized; that is, they are designed by national organizations to be applicable to a large population and to measure a given level of accomplishment. Challenge exams are not standardized. Unlike standardized national exams, challenge exams may reflect the particular philosophy or interests of the professor who teaches the course and may be based on the textbook for that course. Therefore, a bit of caution is in order. Before making a decision to take a challenge exam, it's wise to review the textbook used in the course and discuss the material to be covered with the teacher.

8. *Oral Examinations.* Colleges will sometimes require that a faculty member review and evaluate your learnings in an interview situation. An oral examination may be highly structured or quite informal. Some faculty will ask you a number of previously prepared questions; others may prefer to simply engage you in a discussion of the subject at hand so that they may determine the depth and breadth of your learning. Like challenge exams, oral exams are not standardized and tend to be dependent upon the particular course the instructor is teaching. Discuss this option with your advisor before pursuing a college-based oral exam.

9. *Professional Certifying Examinations.* These are designed and administered by organizations that want to give their members a means of recognition for their skills. Such exams exist in various educational, social service, business, and technical fields. They may or may not cover equivalent college-level skills and learning, but if you have taken and passed such exams you may wish to include them in your portfolio for faculty review.

For further information about the scope of standardized exams and for addresses of sponsoring organizations, see appendix E.

You've probably heard someone say, "I test poorly," or "I'm not a good test taker." It's true that some people do freeze up when they're asked to take paper and pencil tests; they get nervous and can't do their best. You can learn to be a better test taker, however. If you think that testing is the most efficient way for you to earn credit for what you know, but are nervous about your test taking abilities, you can probably get help from your school's academic counselors or basic skills teachers. They can give you some simple techniques that will help you do your best, including such pointers as whether to fill in all answers or to leave blanks when you're uncertain of the right answer. A librarian can also help you find books or articles on how best to approach test taking. Finally, if you plan to take the CLEP or ACT-PEP tests, your bookstore will have books with sample copies of these tests on which you can practice.

▲ Credit for the Completion of Evaluated Programs

Much of the formal adult education and training in the United States takes place in courses sponsored by the military, by corporations and unions, and by such government agencies as the Department of Agriculture. Some of these courses are taught by experts in the field, cover the material in depth, and are highly demanding. If you have taken such a course, your learning may be appropriate for college credit and should be assessed.

There may be a shortcut, however. There are national organizations that evaluate such courses and make credit recommendations. If the course or courses you took have already been evaluated, colleges which accept such recommendations will ask you for evidence or documentation that you actually took the course. If the documentation is satisfactory, you will not have to take a test or oral examination. Following are the main sources of information on evaluated programs:

Guide for the Program on Non-Collegiate Sponsored Instruction (PONSI). Sponsored by the American Council on Education (ACE), the recommendations of which are widely accepted, PONSI evaluations have been done on several hundred corporate training programs as well as a number of union and government programs. You can find out whether a program you took has been evaluated by looking it up in the PONSI guide in your local library or in the library of the school you are planning to attend.

A Guide to the Evaluation of Educational Experiences in the Armed Services, American Council on Education. Military personnel frequently complete the equivalent of college courses while in the service. These include:

▲ formal service school courses

▲ correspondence courses with proctored end-of-the-course examinations

▲ Department of Defense (DOD) courses

▲ Army military occupation specialties

▲ Navy general rates and ratings

A record of these should appear on your discharge papers. If you are uncertain about the status of courses you took while in the service, you can look them up in the ACE Guide or ask the registrar at the school of your choice to review your records of military education. You will need your military discharge papers, DD214, as documentation.

You may also have taken a television, radio or newspaper course or a correspondence course that was sponsored by a college and therefore has already been evaluated. It may require some investigating on your part, but it's well worth your time and effort to learn as much as you can about each of these potentially credit-bearing opportunities.

▲ Credit for Professional Licenses or Certificates

If you are a licensed practical nurse, real estate broker, detective, pilot, vocational education teacher, or some other profession that has testing requirements, or if you have completed an apprenticeship in the automotive, building, or other trades, you may find that getting credit for what you have learned is made easier. Some colleges have recognized specific professional credentials and licenses as representing a fixed amount of college-level learning, and in those colleges, mechanisms for granting college credit are already in place. In such a case, it is a fairly simple matter to "prove" that you have the credential. The assessment counselor or head of the assessment program at the school of your choice should be able to tell you if your particular license or credential has already been evaluated.

▲ Sample Applications of Assessment Methods

All of these methods of assessment may be used alone or as part of your portfolio-assisted assessment. Let's look at how some of the people in the profiles in chapter 2 have approached making choices among assessment modes.

Scott's learnings, though extensive and varied, do not fit easily into standard test categories, nor were any of them acquired through formal company-sponsored training that might have been evaluated. Therefore, he has chosen to assemble a portfolio that will describe and document his learning.

Joan's background includes a mixture of conventional and highly individualized learning. She plans to take two of the general CLEP exams, English and humanities, based on her ability to write well and on her general knowledge about literature, music and art. In addition, she will take the DANTES exam on counseling, which she thinks may reflect what she learned in her work with Alcoholics Anonymous. She will incorporate the outcomes of these exams, along with descriptions and documentation for her other learnings in art, film, and community organization, into a portfolio.

Scott's learnings, though extensive and varied, do not fit easily into standard test categories. Therefore, he has chosen to assemble a portfolio that will describe and document his learning.

Dorene has had a difficult time deciding among the many assessment options open to her. Her present plans are to take the CLEP subject exam in College Spanish, Levels 1 and 2. She is also going to find out whether the company-sponsored courses she took in word processing and data base management have been evaluated. If not, she will also take the CLEP exam in Information Systems and Computer Applications (one test).

In order to evaluate her considerable office skills, she is investigating the tests given by Professional Secretaries International (PSI) through its Institute for Certifying Secretaries. She feels that she may be able to pass the tests on behavioral science in business, office technology, and communication applications.

Dorene's union-sponsored courses in labor relations and labor history are listed in the PONSI guide as recommended for credit, so she expects to receive credit for them.

Because of the variety of her learnings and her need to weave this all together into a coherent package, Dorene plans to develop a portfolio that will incorporate the results of tests and evaluated programs, along with descriptions and documentation of her learnings in computer applications and Puerto Rican politics and literature.

Max has already taken and passed the five general CLEP tests. Now he is looking into whether the company-sponsored courses he took while working on the assembly line of a car manufacturing company have been evaluated in the PONSI guide. He will also consult the ACE Guide to the Evaluation of Educational Experiences in the Armed Services to see whether any of the courses he took before being sent to Vietnam are listed.

Max feels that his counseling work with the black youth group and his knowledge of music theory and performance should be evaluated by representatives of the departments of social work and music at his college of choice, so he plans to incorporate all of his learnings into a portfolio.

It was difficult for her college counselor to convince **Anna** that she had learned anything at all on her own that was worth college credit. Initially she just kept saying that she was a housewife and didn't know anything that was worth college credit. However, now that she has accepted the idea that she is an accomplished learner, a gifted cook, and an able administrator, she is busy making lists of her learnings and is beginning to assemble documentation for them.

Anna is terrified of tests, so even though she has been told she could probably pass a test on child psychology, and possibly in English and social studies as well, she plans to present all of her learnings through portfolio-assisted assessment.

CHAPTER

7

Portfolio-Assisted Assessment

Nothing ever becomes real till it is experienced.
John Keats

In the previous chapter we talked about some of the ways in which adults can earn college credit for their prior learning through presenting documents (transcripts and/or apprenticeship records, records of military or corporate training courses evaluated by the American Council for Education) or through taking tests (CLEP, ACT-PEP, DANTES, Job Ready Level Assessment, challenge exams, etc.). However, not all kinds of valid learning are recorded on transcripts or can be measured by standardized tests. Learning acquired outside the classroom may have been accumulated over an extended period of time or in a number of different situations, and there may be no easily obtainable "proof" that you have acquired it. Moreover, since extra-collegiate learning frequently does not fall into neatly labeled categories, there may be no standardized exams that address exactly what you have learned. Many schools, seeking a way to validate the knowledge and competencies gained by adults outside the classroom, have adopted **portfolio-assisted assessment** as a reliable and flexible way of enabling people to define and explain the learning they have gained from experience and to give evidence of the validity of that learning.

▲ What Is a Portfolio?

A portfolio is a formal written communication, presented by the student to the college, requesting credit or recognition for extra-collegiate learning. The portfolio must make its case by identifying learning clearly and succinctly, and it must provide sufficient supporting information and documentation so that faculty can use it, alone or in combination with other evidence, as the basis for their evaluation.

In addition to the portfolio's immediate use for gaining credit for learning through assessment, it can also be an invaluable document as the student applies for jobs or further educational opportunities. Moreover, most people find that their portfolio becomes a very precious personal record of their accomplishments as learning adults.

In recent years the portfolio concept has been expanded and adapted to such varying uses as documenting the growth of skills and knowledge in school children from kindergarten to twelfth grade; to demonstrating skills and competencies in job situations; as a tool for measurement and evaluation in various academic and professional contexts; and, in some cases, as an alternative to the graduate thesis. In all of these situations, the process of creating a portfolio demands that the student be self-directed, committed to the task, and able to carry it out independently, with a minimum of hand-holding.

Remember, **colleges award credit not for the experiences you have had but for the learning**. If you were named athlete of the year, or won a promotion to sales manager over ten other applicants, or successfully completed an Outward Bound course, that is undoubtedly a source of considerable satisfaction to you, but it represents an experience. What you must demonstrate to a college assessor is what *skills or learning* preceded or resulted from that experience. The portfolio gives you the opportunity to do just that.[1]

▲ Parts of the Portfolio

Although the specific requirements for a portfolio may vary somewhat from school to school, they almost all have certain standard elements in common. These are:

1. *Identification and definition* of specific prior learning for which college credit is being requested, including competency statements in each area of knowledge;

2. *An essay or narrative* explaining how this prior learning relates to the student's projected degree program, from what experiences it was gained, and how it fits into his or her overall education and career plans;

3. *Documentation* or evidence that the student has actually acquired the learning he or she is claiming; and

4. *A credit request* listing exactly how much credit the student is asking for in each subject or area.

▲ Identification and Definition of Prior Experiential Learning

This first section of your portfolio should begin with an annotated list of those potentially college-level learnings that you have acquired both through classroom experiences beyond high school, through formal training or experience at work, in the armed services, through hobbies or reading or travel, or in any of the varied ways in which people learn. You might reread the section, "You as a Learner," chapter 5, to refresh your memory on some of the learnings you have already identified.

---

[1] Although putting together a portfolio can be a complicated and even difficult task, there is help available to you beyond the pages of this book. Schools which have portfolio-assisted assessment also have counselors familiar with the system whose job it is to assist you. Many schools also have portfolio workshops, credit or noncredit, in which you can learn more about the process and get help in putting together a document that will reflect your own skills and competencies.

Your portfolio should begin with an annotated list of those potentially college-level learnings that you have acquired through classroom experiences beyond high school, through formal training or experiences at work, through the armed services, or through hobbies, reading, or travel, or in any of the other ways in which people learn.

One way to begin is to prepare an informal learning resume—a chronological list of your jobs and other learning experiences, including a description of exactly what you had to know or be able to do in order to function in those experiences. The list will probably start after high school and go up to the present. Take time to think about your past, review what you have learned and where you have learned it. (See "Prior Learning Checklist," appendix F.)

You might start with your standard work resume, if you have one, or with a list of the jobs you have held. What were your job titles? What were your responsibilities in each job? What did you do on the job, and what did you have to know to do those things? If you were a line supervisor in a small parts factory, how many people reported to you or for how many people were you responsible? What exactly were those responsibilities? What did you have to know about the manufacturing process to do your job? About the product? About union rules? About getting along with people? Were you responsible for maintenance of the machinery? What else were you supposed to do?

Then go on to non-job experiences that have involved learning: hobbies or sports such as soccer or hunting or photography or raising tropical fish; taking care of your family; creative activities such as painting, making pottery or playing an instrument; time in military service; community activities such as volunteer work in a hospital or nursing home, counseling, delivering meals on wheels; intellectual pursuits such as reading history or philosophy, writing articles or stories, doing biology experiments on your own. What did you learn? How did you learn it? What were you able to do?

Sometimes just "naming" your learnings can be difficult. Learning gained through experience isn't always "neat," and people's skills and competencies aren't always gained in the same logical sequence that college professors use to structure their courses. In each case, the challenge is to go beyond what you actually did in any specific activity or area, to what you had to have learned in order to do it. That is, if you say you can "manage" a high school football team, what does that mean? What skills or knowledge are called for in "managing" a high school football team? Here are some suggestions, which you may or may not think are part of managing:

knowledge of the rules of football

understanding of each team player's capabilities, weaknesses and strengths, psychological makeup

ability to schedule a season that pits your team against comparable teams

ability to schedule try outs, practice sessions, periods of rest

first aid ability

understanding of group psychology and how to make a group function effectively as a team

ability to design strategies and new plays

ability to work well with academic teachers, advisers, and administrators

ability to handle or delegate issues relating to finance, personnel, public relations, ticket sales, etc.

This list could go on and on. Managing a high school football team turns out to be an extraordinarily complicated job, involving a number of different kinds of learning. Moreover, since most schools don't teach a course called "Managing Football Teams," these learnings would probably end up by being listed under more conventional course-related headings, such as physical education, psychology, and management.

Let's look at the people in our profiles to see what kinds of learning lists they might produce.[2]

Scott A. originally said that he had "no real learning to speak of," certainly nothing that a college might be interested in. After a conversation with the assessment counselor at the local community college, however, he began to look with more respect at what he has learned.

Scott's experience with the lumber industry has been a source of considerable learning about forestry: he knows how to operate and maintain the heavy machinery involved in cutting and transport-

---

[2] Scott's list, as well as the others that follow, assumes that he has already begun to talk to a college assessment counselor and is therefore trying to express his learnings in terms of roughly equivalent college courses.

ing lumber; from the time he spent in the seed orchards, he knows how to plant new trees (the best species, desirable soil and geographical conditions, maintenance) and understands the concept of reforestation; he has learned something about the economy of timbering and, through 18 months spent at the company's paper mill, has an understanding of the process of turning wood into paper. Both from workshops sponsored by the company and from his experience in the field, Scott has also learned a great deal about logging safety.

Like many of the people in his part of the country, Scott is a savvy bass fisherman who has learned where to look for fish in different river and weather conditions, how to choose bait, place his cast, and haul in the fish without breaking his line, but he didn't think this was worth mentioning until his assessment counselor told him that the physical education department of the local community college offers a beginner's course in fishing for which he might be eligible for credit.

Through Scott's Bible study group, he has gained an extensive knowledge of both the Old and New Testaments and has begun to understand that they have a historical, religious and literary significance that goes beyond the literal text. He has led the group in its Bible discussions for about three years, and feels that he has learned some important things not only about his own religion but beyond his church's interpretation of the texts. He has also studied the origin of religious texts as well as how to prepare for leading group discussions. He was encouraged to list these learnings for possible evaluation by a member of the school's religion and philosophy department.

Scott's hobby is making furniture. His tables and desks are much in demand in his local community, and last year he won first prize in a local crafts show for a birch end table that he had both designed and made. The school he is planning to attend offers a few crafts courses in making pottery and jewelry, but none in furniture making. Scott has been encouraged by his assessment counselor to ask the head of the crafts program if his skills in furniture making might be eligible for credit.

A list of Scott's learning experiences is shown in Exhibit 7-1.

▲ **Exhibit 7-1:** Scott's Learning Experiences

Source, Date	Nature of Experience	Description of Scott's Learnings
Perkins' Grocery, part-time 1959–1961	Stocking boy	▲ Knows how to stock shelves, putting older items in front, straightening them for neatness, marking prices accurately, checking invoices against merchandise
Eureka Paper Co., 1962–present	Logging	▲ Knows how to drive, use, maintain heavy machinery (skidders, tractors, logging trucks, de-limbers, chain saws)
		▲ Reforestation: knows desirable soil and terrain conditions; planting, thinning, harvesting techniques; principles of forest ecology
		▲ Teamwork: knows how to get along with other members of work team, problem solve, cooperate with management
		▲ Logging safety: knows OSHA regulations
1971–1973	Working in Eureka's paper mill	▲ Knows production line techniques, chemistry of paper making, technology of paper making

Source, Date	Nature of Experience	Description of Scott's Learnings
Union Methodist Church, 1978–present	Participating in and leading Bible discussion group	◄ Knows Old and New Testaments; historical, religious, literary significance of Bible
Hobby, 1955–present	Fishing	◄ Has skill in casting, fly tying, catching/landing the fish ◄ Knows fish habitat, best weather and water conditions ◄ Has skill in boat handling, knows local waters
Hobby, 1970–present	Designing and making furniture	◄ Has skill in basic carpentry and woodworking ◄ Knows properties of different varieties of wood ◄ Knows finishing and refinishing techniques ◄ Knows some principles of furniture design ◄ Knowledgeable about 19th-century American furniture, its construction and design

Joan B.'s prior learning list is very different from Scott's, but, like him, she found that it included a lot of learning that she had always taken for granted without realizing that it might be similar to what colleges were teaching.

In order to become a docent at the local art museum, Joan had gone through a six-month training period with the director of the museum and his staff. During that time, she not only became familiar with the major periods of art covered in the museum's collection but learned how to do oral presentations for groups of tourists and students.

After this first phase of their training was complete, each docent was asked to choose one period of art in which to specialize, doing extensive reading and viewing of slides and other collections in that period and writing a research paper. Joan chose to specialize in Egyptian art. As part of her research, she read books and articles about ancient Egyptian history, culture and architecture. She learned enough hieroglyphics to be able to read some of the inscriptions on the tombs and monuments, and she wrote a paper on the monuments of the Upper Nile. When the museum director realized how knowledgeable Joan had become in Egyptology, he asked her to give a talk in the evening public lecture series and invited her to consult with the museum librarian about increasing their holdings in visual and print materials on Egypt.

Joan's experience in working with a friend on a film about Artists in the City was also a rich source of learnings about how to write a script, direct the actors and camera people and other technicians, and produce a low budget film that was good enough to be shown in a number of high schools throughout the city.

In her efforts to save her marriage by helping her alcoholic husband conquer his addiction, Joan had become familiar with the physical and emotional dimensions of substance abuse, and through reading and involvement with Alcoholics Anonymous, she learned how group process works to help the addict. For the past few years, Joan has been leading an Al Anon group, for which she prepares by extensive reading in the theory of group interaction and attendance at leadership seminars sponsored by the church.

Joan's first attempt at listing her learnings is shown in Exhibit 7-2.

When her college assessment counselor first asked **Dorene G.** to list those learnings acquired on the job or through other experience, she resisted, saying that she had learned her office skills in high school and didn't know anything in which a college would be interested. However, when the counselor encouraged her to talk about what she did, Dorene soon realized that her extensive competence in a number of business functions went far beyond her own high school learning and beyond that of anyone else in her office. She had become proficient in word processing, knew how to use spreadsheets, and had taught herself desktop publishing. She was not only responsible for teaching word processing to new clerical staff but was in charge of designing systems to manage the flow of computer information and was responsible for making decisions about new hardware and software purchases for the office.

Dorene's union activities turned out to be a rich source of learning. Based on the union courses she took, as well as on her actual experience of participating as a union representative in the last two rounds of bargaining with her company, she included contract negotiation in her learning list. She also completed a union-sponsored course in the history of labor relations in the United States, which she thinks covers the same material as the local college's course in that subject.

Neither Dorene nor her counselor are yet ready to predict that her learnings in Puerto Rican history, politics, language and literature will be considered college level or will be equivalent to any college department's offerings. Nevertheless, she has included knowledge of the Puerto Rican statehood movement and Latin American literature in her list of learnings, and she is continuing to study from Spanish language tapes and to read further in the literature of her grandparents' native country.

Max W.'s work in the automobile industry has given him a rich background in basic automotive maintenance, engine diagnosis and tune-up, automotive engines and electrical systems, and automotive welding techniques that will probably give him a head start toward an associate's degree in automotive technology.

However, Max has also gained other knowledge and competencies that will enable him to gain credit in non-automotive areas so as to broaden his degree program. During Max's many years of volunteer work with a black community youth group, he attended

▲ **Exhibit 7-2:** Joan's Learning Experiences

Source, Date	Nature of Experience	Description of Joan's Learnings
Morse College	Attended college for one semester (12 credits)	▲ Studied English composition, European history, music appreciation and organic chemistry
Art galleries, art journals, 1964–present	Reading and observing	▲ Knows work of major modern painters and sculptors; can discuss characteristics of major contemporary schools of art; is familiar with terminology, media
Dance recitals, books and films on modern dance, 1968–present	Reading and observing	▲ Knows and understands techniques of modern dance; characteristics of modern dancers, directors and companies
Fine Arts Museum 1987–1988	Attended training program, three days per week for six month	▲ Learned about major periods of western art, major artists ▲ Did research on Egyptian art—learned about period, styles, media, relationship of art to culture, research techniques, how to organize and write a research paper ▲ Learned to organize and present a lecture on art to a group of people ▲ Learned about the scope of a museum's collection, and how decisions are made about buying and de-accessioning

Source, Date	Nature of Experience	Description of Joan's Learnings
Making a film with friends, 1985–1986	Collaborated on script writing, directing, financing	▲ Learned how to write film script, principles of film directing, production techniques, marketing and public relations
Alcoholics Anonymous, 1984–1988	Participated as wife of alcoholic, reading about addiction	▲ Learned about physical and psychological aspects of substance abuse, how group dynamics work, spouse's role in helping an addict
Al Anon, 1988–1989	Led Al Anon group	▲ Learned group dynamics, the responsibilities of a leader, how to deal with participants' stress, how to control own emotions

a number of church seminars designed to help youth group leaders function more effectively. These seminars, plus his actual experience with young people and the considerable background reading he did, may very possibly have given him college-level learning in leadership skills, group process and adolescent psychology.

Max is also an accomplished trumpet player and feels he has the equivalent of at least two college music performance courses. He has put this down on his learnings list, but as the community college he plans to attend teaches music appreciation but not performance, it is not yet clear whether they will agree to evaluate his ability to play an instrument. He has, however, found a course on jazz theory in the college catalog that covers approximately what he knows. He also thinks his knowledge of classical music and theory may be equivalent to what is taught in an introductory music appreciation course.

When Max first talked to the college assessment counselor, he did not even mention the job with which he partially supported himself for the first five years after high school. He sold tickets and ran the projector at a local movie house that specialized in old and foreign films. This job did not at first seem to involve significant learnings beyond using his elementary school arithmetic to make change plus using the modest amount of mechanical ability needed to load the projector and perform routine jobs running the projector and doing basic maintenance. The movie house owner had taught him these in a few hours, and Max was pretty sure that they were not college level. But when the counselor asked him why he had stayed for so long in a low paying job, Max enthusiastically explained that he had become fascinated by the movies he ran and had begun reading about film making and film history. In his spare time he went to the local community college's film library, where he was able to view important early films and to follow the progress of certain directors whose techniques fascinated him. Since that time, Max's interest in film has continued, and he spends a lot of his leisure time going to the movies and reading film journals. In fact, when Max looked at the course descriptions in the community college's Communications Department, he realized that his knowledge of film history was easily equivalent to what he could have learned in the classroom. Exhibit 7-3 lists Max's learning experiences.

Anna P. had a difficult time assembling her list of learnings. A modest woman, she found it hard to believe that the things she

▲ Exhibit 7-3: Max's Learning Experiences

Source, Date	Nature of Experience	Description of Max's Learnings
Globe Movie Theatre, part-time 1974–1978	Working as assistant projectionist	◢ Knows operation, maintenance of film projectors ◢ Knows American and European films—technique and styles of major directors, understanding of evolution of American film artistry in 20th century
U.S. Coast Guard, 1979–1982	Serving as Seaman 1st Class taking service courses, plus experience	◢ Knows basic seamanship, meteorology, electronics
Major Auto Manufacturer, 1983–present	Apprenticing, working	◢ Knows automotive maintenance, electric systems, welding and painting, parts warehousing (knowledge of inventory procedures, worker supervision, time management)
Hobby, 1973–present	Taking trumpet lessons; playing trumpet in school orchestra, neighborhood rock band; listening to jazz and classical records; reading *Stereo Review*	◢ Plays trumpet at semiprofessional level ◢ Knows classical and jazz music, musical structures, periods ◢ Recognizes major composers and their works
Volunteer Work with Community Youth Group, 1987–present	Working with troubled teenagers, attending church-sponsored workshops on counseling	◢ Has ability to command attention and respect of teenage boys; understands teenage problems with sex, drugs, schools, family; can help troubled kids; works successfully with individual kids and with groups

knew and could do, which she took very much for granted, could be worth college credit. An understanding counselor spent considerable time with Anna, teasing out descriptions of her learnings and equating them to college level learning. The counselor also helped Anna to see that there is value attached to learning derived from work, regardless of whether that work was paid or done on a volunteer basis. Because Anna is a thoughtful person who deliberates, reads, attends workshops and seminars, and consults other people before she acts, it turned out that she could demonstrate in-depth learnings in a variety of areas. She understands theories of child development and has had the practical experience of taking care of her own children and the children of others. She had prepared thoroughly for her work with the local cancer society through reading, observation, and discussion with the leaders of other organizations. And in her leadership role there, she had made herself thoroughly familiar with the financial aspects of the organization, had handled the corps of volunteers with skill and diplomacy, and had managed a shrewd public relations campaign that made each year's fund drive more successful than the last.

Anna was not only a superb cook, but her culinary skills were also based on both practice and a knowledge of the basic principles of nutrition and the chemistry of cooking.

▲ College-Level Learning

As you can see, the learning experiences of our five profiled friends cover a wide range of territory. Some occurred in college courses and will be recorded on a transcript (Joan). Some were the result of time in the armed services (Max), formal company or union-sponsored training (Max, Dorene and Scott), informal on-the-job experience (Scott, Max and Dorene), volunteer work (Anna and Max), or non-job hobbies and interests (all five).

Some jobs, like Max's as projectionist, may have offered learning experiences that aren't immediately apparent. So take your time going over your own past history to discover learning experiences. You don't have to finish your list all at one time. Give yourself a chance to reflect on what you have done in your lifetime and what you have learned. The forms in appendices F and G may be helpful in organizing your list.

Don't ignore those learnings that at first glance don't seem to have much to do with what is taught in college. Remember, colleges have physical education departments that may have courses in such sports as tennis, soccer, and swimming. They have sociology or social work departments that may have courses in drug or alcohol counseling, or group therapy. They have psychology and education departments that almost certainly teach early childhood development or the psychology of teenagers.

Keep in mind, however, that not all of what Max, Joan, Scott, Dorene, and Anna have learned (or what you have learned) is necessarily appropriate for inclusion in a final portfolio. Scott's early experience in a grocery store taught him a lot about responsibility and gave him some fundamental understanding of product stocking and display, but it did not result in any college level learnings. Before preceding any further, remember that if you are requesting college credit you must describe your learning in such a way that it meets the following criteria.

College level learning must:

▲ be measurable;

▲ be at a level of achievement defined by the faculty as college equivalent or consistent with the learning of other students engaged in college studies;

▲ be applicable outside the specific job or context in which it was learned;

▲ have a knowledge base;

▲ be reasonably current;

▲ imply a conceptual or theoretical as well as a practical understanding;

▲ show some relationship to your degree goals and/or lifelong learning goals; and

▲ not repeat learning for which credit has already been awarded.

The school you are planning to attend can help you determine the "fit" between your learning and these criteria.

After you have made your initial list of learnings and given yourself a few days or weeks to think about them (and perhaps to add more), you are ready to put together your first version of the formal list of learning components that will actually go into your portfolio. While schools may have different formats for this, the form used by Scott, Max, and Joan will be sufficient to get you started in assembling your critical information in a way that is clear and easily understandable. Eventually you will need to go back to your list, decide which learning components are potentially college level, and find ways to describe them in greater detail so that they will clearly satisfy the eligibility requirements for college credit listed above.

For example, with the help of her assessment counselor, Joan realized that in her work as a docent, she had become quite competent as a public speaker and that her learnings, if fully described, probably covered much of what is taught in Speech 101. Joan's final definition of her learnings in Speech looked like this:

I can overcome nervousness when talking to groups by making certain that I know the material thoroughly; making eye contact with my audience; checking out my audiovisual equipment ahead of time so that I'm not embarrassed by a non-functioning projector or burnt out bulb.

To make a presentation sound natural, I prepare thoroughly, but speak from an outline, not a written out or memorized speech; I relate information from my own experience; I use natural gestures and employ humor; when asked questions, I invite audience comment.

To make certain that the information I provide about the paintings and sculpture comes across accurately and holds the audience's attention, I start with ideas or facts that are particularly interesting; I relate each period, artist, or object to something they are likely to already know about; I make clear connections among the various periods, artists, and objects; when I want to emphasize a point, I repeat it, using different words.

I make certain that my audience can hear me without straining; I have listened to myself speak on video and have learned how to modulate my voice; I make smooth transitions from one topic to another; I stop frequently to encourage audience comment and to respond to it; I try to frame questions that will provoke discussion and that go beyond a simple yes or no answer.

I welcome criticism and accept it gracefully.

▲ The Essay or Narrative

Most assessment programs require that a general essay or narrative be included in the portfolio in which you tell something about yourself, your experiences, your goals and aspirations, and your reasons for seeking credit for your prior learning. This essay should also show how your present learnings are linked to what you plan to study in college, and, in some cases, should include mention of what you haven't yet learned—the gaps in your knowledge and skills that you want to fill in through further education.

Some schools may ask you to do a series of shorter essays supporting each competence area. That is, if you were requesting credit in business management, electronics, and Civil War history, you would do a brief essay explaining your learnings in each of these areas—how you acquired them, a description of the depth and breadth of your knowledge or skills, how they relate to college level learning (see above, p. 99), and how they fit in with your general degree program.[3]

Although the essay or narrative is frequently not linked as strongly to the actual credit recommendations as is your documentation, it is a very important component because it communicates *who* you are. College students who attend classes usually have an entire 15-week semester to convey to their professors who they are. Through classroom participation, promptness in completing assignments, performance in research projects and exams, professors get a pretty good idea of their students' motivation, breadth and quality of knowledge, and the level of their communication skills. In most assessment of prior learning programs, you are expected to accomplish all of this through your portfolio and perhaps an evaluation interview with a faculty member in each of your learning areas.

Clearly, the essay is a major opportunity to introduce yourself to the people who will be making final judgments about the validity of your credit requests. A good essay can convey information about

---

[3] *Descriptions of your learning components will be the heart of your portfolio.* Depending on your college's preferred outline, they will appear either in the narrative essay or (preferably) in conjunction with your credit requests and support documentation.

your motivation, competence, and communications skills. It will also help you put your knowledge and experience in perspective.

Although your own institution, if it requires an essay, will probably provide you with its own outline, here are a few suggestions for developing this part of your portfolio.

1. *Begin in a straightforward manner*, that is, state your goals and relate them to your reasons for seeking credit for your prior learning.

2. *Tell enough about your life so that the assessor gets a sense of who you are and where you are going.* A **brief** autobiography is a way of conveying your background, your interests, and your personality. While it is not usually appropriate to write about the intimate details of your growing up or your marriage, or your various illnesses, sometimes these things bear directly on your motivation for learning or going back to school. If so, include them, but keep them short and to the point. Don't turn the autobiography into a confessional orgy! Remember, it will become a public document and will be read by strangers.

3. *Use a tone that is self-confident and assertive.* You want to communicate your strengths and accomplishments and also give the reader a sense of your motivation. Are you completing something started long ago or seeking a job promotion? Whatever the motivating factor is for you to want to earn credits through the assessment process, let it come across in your tone.

    The most impressive essays or narratives convey not only the factors that have contributed to a person's experience or growth, but also some sense of excitement about continuing that experience or growth in a new direction, with greater understanding and motivation.

4. *Organize your essay or narrative in a clear, logical, and comfortable way.* You may wish to do this chronologically (by time sequence) or by subject matter; whatever "feels" right to you will probably produce the best results.

5. *Be sure that you are addressing what is important to your institution.* Some institutions seek full autobiographies; others consider only the learning experiences directly related to your request for credit. Read carefully the description of the essay that your institution uses in its portfolio assessment literature, and make certain that you include everything it considers relevant.

6. *Develop a conclusion.* Make sure that the end of your essay or narrative sums up why you are seeking to earn credits through portfolio-assisted assessment, and what this will mean to your future. Although there is no formula for a perfect conclusion, you will want to make certain yours is consistent with the rest of your text and is positive in tone.

7. *Edit, edit, edit.* Get an early start on the essay so that you can put the first draft away for a while, and then, when you can approach it afresh and see your mistakes, rewrite it. Not even Hemingway tried to publish his first drafts.

   It may also help to have a friend who writes well or a former teacher look the essay over to make certain that there are no obvious grammatical or spelling errors and, even more important, that it says what you mean it to say.

Don't be intimidated at the prospect of writing an essay. Although many adults approach it as a difficult task, it can be one of the most rewarding experiences of the assessment process. The essay offers you a unique opportunity to reflect upon your past, gain a new understanding of yourself and all you've accomplished in your life, and anticipate with confidence your future plans and objectives.

▲ Documenting Your Skills and Knowledge

The purpose of the documentation section of your portfolio is to provide evidence of your having acquired the learnings described in your portfolio. Just as students in a classroom must provide evidence of their learning in the form of book reports, oral presentations, research papers or examination results, so too, you will be expected to demonstrate that you really do possess the knowledge or skills you claim to have.

Documentation may take many forms: a computer program you've designed; an official transcript of a company training course you've taken; a tape of a piano recital you gave; a letter from a former employer outlining your job responsibilities and describing your performance. In this section, we will look at different kinds of documentation you may be able to use and discuss how best to obtain that documentation.

Documentation Resources

No doubt when you were listing your work and learning activities, you recalled specific people, projects, or reports that were critical to your success. These could serve as your documentation resources. In fact, it would be useful to go back to that form and add a column on the right in which you can list possible documentation for each learning component.

Documentation resources usually fall into two categories: direct and indirect. **Direct documentation** refers to products you have produced, performances you have given, reports you have written, marketing plans you have produced, etc. In most cases, direct documentation serves as the strongest evidence that you really do know what you say you know or have the skills you say you have. You must be prepared to prove, however, that the evidence or product was created by you.

Examples of **direct documentation** include:

▲ management reports you have compiled and written, in whole or in part

▲ photographs you have taken

▲ articles, plays, poems, or stories you have written

▲ audio or audiovisual tapes of speeches, talks, training or performances you have given

▲ blueprints of electronic circuits or buildings you have designed

▲ musical scores you have arranged

▲ computer programs you have designed

▲ manuals or brochures you have written or designed

▲ patents you have obtained

▲ curriculum plans you have prepared

▲ paintings, sculptures, or drawings you have created

In all of these forms of direct documentation, there must be some form of validation that the photograph or tape or computer program is really yours or a clear indication of the part you actually played in the preparation of the whole. Original signatures, printed acknowledgements, accompanying letters of confirmation, etc. may provide that validation.

Indirect documentation is usually information *about* you and your accomplishments. It can take the form of:

▲ letters written on your behalf by employers, co-workers, business partners, business consultants, teachers, church, community or government leaders, professional association members

▲ commendations you may have received (awards, medals, official recommendations)

▲ official personnel evaluations by your supervisor

▲ transcripts showing test results or college courses passed or documenting completion of training programs

▲ program notes from performances you have given or exhibits in which you have shown your work

▲ magazine or newspaper articles about you and your accomplishments

Weak sources of documentation, which should be **avoided,** include:

▲ letters from family members, your own students or clients, your own employees, friends who might serve as "personal references" in other contexts

▲ travel brochures of places you have visited

▲ newspaper clippings about events in which you say you participated but which do not mention you

▲ job evaluations that are not specific about what you actually did or what skills you exhibited. An evaluation that merely states you were a good employee, or even a superb employee is poor documentation for your skills and learnings

Documentation Steps

1. Identify what you know.

You can only begin to think about documenting your knowledge after it's been identified. Before requesting or assembling your documentation, be sure you know exactly what learning it is you're trying to verify (refer to the list of learnings that you should have compiled earlier in this chapter). Feel free to consult with the college you are planning to attend for assistance with this process.

2. List your documentation resources.

A. For **direct documentation**, inventory the pieces you plan to use. Do you know where they are? Where did you put your copy of your last personnel evaluation? Is your best painting on the wall in your local library or in your studio? Is a co-worker using your curriculum plan at the vocational school or is a copy in your desk? After you prepare your inventory, organize all the pieces you plan to use in one location.

B. For **indirect documentation**, make a list of all the people who could potentially serve to document your knowledge and abilities. Be as thorough as possible. If you own a small business, you might initially think only of your partner. But what about your attorney, your tax accountant, or your banker? Often two or three letters from different sources that verify the same aspect of your knowledge prove complementary to one other. One writer may emphasize somewhat different aspects of your knowledge or skills than another.

Gather articles about yourself, program notes listing you as a speaker or performer, or letters of commendation you may have received for outstanding work in a volunteer organization. Add these to your documentation resource materials. They're likely to come in handy.

3. Request the documentation you need.

This process may take time, so begin to gather your direct documentation as soon as you begin work on your portfolio. If you need letters from former teachers, supervisors, or co-workers, start assembling your list and find the addresses. (Some schools have form letters they want you to use. If not, see the format of requests for documentation on p. 186.) If you have paintings, architectural drawings, or other pieces of your work out on display or loan, call or write to make arrangements to retrieve them. If the object is too large to retrieve or if it cannot be removed, make arrangements to have high quality photographs or slides made of your work. In the case of written materials, make sure to have duplicate copies made to include in your portfolio.

4. When to request documentation.

Since you will more than likely depend on others to provide you with some of the documentation you need, you want to send your request letters off as soon as possible after you enroll in a portfolio course or begin to work with an assessment counselor. Give your document resource persons a deadline of at least two weeks prior to the time you actually will need their letters. (It would be safer to allow four to six weeks.) After a month, you may wish to follow up your written requests with second phone calls—a gentle reminder that your deadline is fast approaching and an offer to provide any information that will make the job easier for them.

5. Monitor your documentation requests.

To keep track of your document resources (to whom you've written, who has responded, the location of other kinds of documentation), develop a worksheet similar to the one in appendix G. It will help you to organize your direct and indirect documentation and permit you to see at a glance what you still need to do. It will also help you avoid last minute problems. You will need to know three things:

▲ for what courses (or areas of competence) you are seeking credit,

▲ what kind of documentation you need, and

▲ where you can get that documentation.

In the first column on the left, list the course names or areas of competence for which you are requesting credit. Then fill out the types of documentation you need and, if applicable, the names of any people who will provide them. Note the dates you mail the request letters and the dates the answers are received. This will help you place those necessary follow-up calls if more than a month lapses from the time you made your initial request. And finally, to avoid last minute panic, be sure to note *where* each piece of documentation is kept.

To obtain the necessary **indirect documentation**, begin by contacting each person twice—once by phone or in person and again in writing. Explain why you want the documentation, mention the assessment program and the college or university by name, and discuss how the documentation will help you.

Content of Letters of Documentation

Letters of documentation may be from former employers, supervisors, teachers—anyone who has been in a position to know you and judge your work. Remember that it is sometimes very difficult for people to understand **the difference between a letter of recommendation** (which they may have written dozens of times before) **and a letter of documentation** (which is probably a new concept for most people). You are not asking anyone to verify your character or attest to your winning personality. You are asking the people you contact to confirm that you have indeed done what you claim to have done (worked for ACME Widget Factory for six years from 1978–1984), doing the tasks you have said you did, and, most important, demonstrating the learnings you are claiming.

Specify exactly what knowledge you want documented because only documentation that verifies learning can be used to support your claims as to what you know. A letter intended to document learnings should include:

1. Evidence that the person writing the letter is in a position to be knowledgeable about you and the quality of your work or performance. The letterhead, if it includes the person's title, may be sufficient to convey this. If not, the writer should state in what capacity he knew you, e.g., "I was Jeff's supervisor for 5 years in the Acme Widget Factory," or "Jeff and I worked together for six months on the Township's Planning Committee."

2. A detailed summary of your responsibilities or a job description.

3. An explanation of what skills, competencies or knowledge you had to demonstrate in order to fulfill the job responsibilities.

4. An evaluation of your performance on the job, with some indication, if possible, of how that performance might compare to that demanded in a college course. (This last is the most difficult for most people to write, and you may find that you will have to forego this kind of evaluative comment.)

Content of Letters Requesting Documentation

The sample letter on the next page, Exhibit 7-4, which Dorene sent to her supervisor, may be helpful as a model for your own requests. You will want to revise it to fit your personality and make it specific to your needs and circumstances. The more specific you are, the better your chances of getting the document you need.

▲ **Exhibit 7-4**

Ms. Helen Brown, Personnel
A&B Communications, Inc.
125 Main Street, Suite 108
Unionville, AR 55555

Dear Ms. Brown:

As we discussed on the telephone, I am writing to ask you for a letter on my behalf for Unionville College's Portfolio-Assisted Assessment Program. As you know, I am hoping to earn college credits toward my degree for knowledge acquired outside the college classroom. Your letter will help me provide evidence that the knowledge and skills I possess are worthy of college credit.

Following the recommendations specified by the Assessment Program of the College, I would appreciate your writing the letter on company letterhead and including the following:

1. A description of my position with all pertinent past and present experiences included.

2. A mention of your relationship to me (supervisor) and the situations in which you have observed me. Also, please include the dates of your observations and the length of time I worked with you.

3. An indication of my competence, skills and knowledge in word processing, spreadsheets, accounting programs, and computer programming. [Here you would specify what your own competencies, skills, and knowledge areas are, and relate them to the course descriptions for which you are seeking credit.]

4. Evaluate how well I performed using such adjectives as *average, above average, exceptional,* etc. It would also be helpful if your statement included some comparison with others you have known who possess a college degree or college credits and who have held similar positions to mine.

It is important for me to add that what you write should not be a letter of recommendation per se. Rather, the Assessment Program requires that you verify my specific skills, competencies, and knowledge, and evaluate the level of my performance.

I would appreciate your sending this letter on company stationery to my advisor [name] at Unionville College [address]. I would like this letter to reach the advisor no later than [allow at least one month from date you write letter].

Thank you very much for agreeing to write this letter on my behalf. As I am sure you are aware, earning a college degree at this point in my life is very important to me.

If you have questions, please let me know.

Sincerely,
Dorene Diaz Garfield

Some of the answers you receive to your requests for documentation may be fine, others may miss the mark. Following are some samples of both types (Exhibits 7-5, 7-6).

Exhibit 7-5 is not an acceptable letter for Max's portfolio because Mr. Kirchner is giving a character reference, which attests to Max's punctuality, diligence, and generosity in filling in for other employees, but says nothing about Max's skills and knowledge.

▲ **Exhibit 7-5:** An Unacceptable Letter
(Written at Max's Telephoned Request)

Detroit Center Theater
180 Lake Drive
Detroit, Michigan 55555-5555

Dear Assessment Counselor:

I am writing this letter for Max Anthony, who worked in
my movie theatre for a number of years as a projectionist.

Max was a fine employee who was always on time and did
whatever he was asked. He would work extra shifts if
someone was ill, and even filled in for the cashier or usher
if necessary.

I am certain that Max will succeed in whatever work he
attempts because he is very smart and tries his best at
whatever he is doing.

Sincerely,
Jacob Kirchner

After receiving this letter, Max went to visit Mr. Kirchner and
took the time to explain why he needed a different kind of letter
and what kinds of information it should contain (he did not tell
Mr. Kirchner what to say). Mr Kirchner's second letter is shown in
Exhibit 7-6.

▲ **Exhibit 7-6:** An Acceptable Letter

Detroit Center Theater
180 Lake Drive
Detroit, Michigan 55555-5555

Dear Assessment Counselor:

Max A. worked for me from 1979–1984 as projectionist at
my movie theatre. During this time, he learned not only to
load and service the projector but also assumed the
responsibility for all basic maintenance. When we decided
to replace our aging projector, I took Max with me because
he was so knowledgeable about the various models and
capabilities of projectors that I would not have been able to
buy one without his help.

I realized after Max had been working for me for a few
months that he shared my love of the movies. He began
asking my permission to screen old, classical movies when
the theatre was closed, and I would frequently find him
reading film books and journals. Eventually, he knew more
about directors and film history than I did and got my
permission to run a foreign film festival on Thursday nights.
This turned out to be so well attended that the following
year he put together a "History of American Film" festival
that ran for 12 weeks and made more money than our
regular features. We used to play a kind of trivia game in
which we would spring questions about films at each other,
but he almost always won.

I keep kidding Max that anytime he gets tired of making
automobiles, he should come back and be my projectionist.
He was the best I ever had.

Jacob Kirchner

While Exhibit 7-6 is not a perfect letter of validation, it is certainly much better than Mr. Kirchner's first attempt. It does address Max's competence as a projectionist and gives information about his knowledge of film. By itself, however, it could probably not serve as documentation for the six credits Max is requesting in film history and theory since it does not specify the depth and breadth of his knowledge. Although this letter will definitely be included in Max's portfolio, his college will probably also arrange for him to be evaluated by a professor in the film division of the art department.

Dorene G. decided to ask her former employer, Ms. Brown, for a letter that would verify her capabilities in computer applications. She not only wrote her a letter of request (pp. 109–110), she took the time to make an appointment with Ms. Brown and spent about half an hour describing the assessment process and explaining why a letter from her would be a crucial document for Dorene's portfolio. Ms. Brown's letter is shown in Exhibit 7-7.

 Exhibit 7-7: An Excellent Letter

A&B Communications Inc.
125 Main Street, Suite 108
Unionville, AR 55555

To Whom it May Concern:

I was Dorene G's immediate supervisor at A&B Communications for four years. During that time I watched Dorene grow from a novice with the computer to one who could handle almost any task we set for her.

Dorene didn't even know word processing when she came to work, but with the help of a manual and some coaching, she became proficient first in WordStar and later in Word Perfect. Eventually she could handle any length or kind of document, could do footnotes, make intricate formatting changes, and even put the company's enormous mailing system on mail merge.

Dorene also taught herself desktop publishing so that she could do our brochures and personnel announcements. A&B began to get a reputation among its competitors as having the best looking direct mail advertising in the business.

Dorene took a company-sponsored course in Lotus 1-2-3 and then designed a new spreadsheet system for the company. Aware that our billing and accounting procedures were too cumbersome, she advised us to buy a new program, Peachtree, and set up our entire accounts receivable and billing processes on this new program. She taught the bookkeeper to use Peachtree and wrote the data entry protocols that enabled us to switch from our old system to the new.

Dorene became thoroughly familiar with the DOS 3.3 system in use in our office and could do simple programming in Basic.

Based on my own experience in teaching a one-year (6 credit) college course in office technologies (State College, 1985), I would say that Dorene's knowledge far exceeds that which is usually covered in a full year in the classroom and that her skills go well beyond what most of the students in my class attained.

Sincerely,
Helen Brown

Her letter was not only accepted by the college as adequate documentation for Dorene's computer applications skills, it was used as a sample for the model portfolio that the assessment counselor was putting together. The letter accomplishes the following:

1. It explains Ms. Brown's relationship with Dorene and why she was in a position to be able to document her learnings;

2. it gives a detailed description of those learnings; and

3. it attempts to equate Dorene's learnings with what would be taught in the average college course.

The Problem of Knowledge or Competence Without Documentation

There are many areas of knowledge for which people wish to earn college credit but have no documentation of any sort—direct or indirect. Frequent examples are proficiency in languages or the humanities, such as specialized areas of literature, history or philosophy. The person may have done extensive reading and study, but doesn't know how to prove it. A reading list, though useful, cannot in itself serve as documentation. In these cases, if a student has no documentation and if there are no standardized credit-by-examination opportunities in his/her area of expertise, colleges will frequently arrange for a special evaluation by a selected faculty member in the field. Indeed, many colleges routinely insist on a faculty evaluation of any knowledge or skill for which there is no transcript or recognized authority, even if you have adequate documentation.

Faculty evaluators are chosen because their areas of specialization cover the knowledge or skills for which you are requesting credit. They may assess your knowledge through an interview (formal or informal), an oral exam, a written examination, or a combination of these methods. The results of this evaluation supplement or occasionally take the place of documentation in your portfolio. Similarly, if you are seeking credit in an area such as the performing arts, laboratory science, or counseling, you may be expected to undergo a performance evaluation. In any of these cases, speak with someone in the assessment program as to your options—there are many ways to get the credit you deserve.

A Word of Caution

Avoid overkill. When assembling documentation, don't succumb to the temptation to clean your attic. If you have to deliver your portfolio in a wheelbarrow, you've overdone it.

In other words, be discriminating in what you include as documentation, **using only those pieces of evidence that are directly**

connected to your credit request. For instance, you may have edited the church newspaper for ten years, but the assessor doesn't have the time to wade through your bound volume of 120 issues of the newspaper. You should present a letter from a church official capable of validating your work and evaluating your editing capacity, and perhaps one or two sample editions of the paper in which your name is listed as editor.

Portfolios filled with bits and pieces of scrapbook items from a person's entire life not only take too long to read, they tend to be confusing and may work against rather than for you.

▲ Determining Your Credit Request

One of your toughest tasks in the assessment process is to figure out how much credit it is appropriate to request. Fortunately, you will most likely have a lot of help in doing this from the assessment counselor or other officials in the college responsible for helping you assemble your portfolio. The following approaches are commonly used, although you must make certain which your school prefers to be sure you are on the right track.

College Course Method

If your college, or the program in which you are enrolled, requires you to match your knowledge to specific college courses, much of the burden of requesting the right amount of credit will be lifted from your shoulders. A quick perusal of that college's catalog will show you how much credit is awarded for successful completion of the courses that most closely approximate what you have learned. If you believe that you can demonstrate comparable knowledge through the assessment process, you should request a like amount of credit.

Matching courses to learnings is not always easy, however. What you've learned on your own may not quite fit the way learning is divided into courses. For example, let us suppose that you have a great deal of practical experience in installing and repairing electrical appliances, have worked alongside an electrician in wiring your new home, and have assembled and customized your own sound system. Here is a typical description of a course in General Electricity:

General Electricity: 3 credits

Studies basic principles of electricity, laws, theories, devices, instruments and testing equipment. Emphasizes direct and alternating current circuits and devices. An examination of electron theory, resistance, inductance, and capacitance allows the student to analyze and generalize as to the behavior and characteristics of electric current. Laboratory experiences allow students to experiment and apply their learnings to problem solving situations.

You must ask yourself honestly whether you have the theoretical knowledge implicit in this description. Perhaps you estimate you know about two-thirds of the course content. Some colleges would allow you to explain that in the portfolio and ask for two credits rather than three. Or perhaps you are confident that you know everything but "capacitance." You might consider reviewing a textbook on electronics and studying the section on capacitance before submitting your portfolio. Or you might consider other possibilities, like adjusting the title from General Electricity to Practical Electronics and adjusting the description to more accurately reflect your learnings.

It is also important to learn whether or not your institution limits the kinds of courses for which you may earn credit. The questions below will help you to gather this information:

Must the courses selected for assessment be from your institution's catalog?

If the descriptions can be from other college catalogs, are there particular limitations or restrictions you need to know?

Can the courses presented for assessment be in your major area, or does the college limit credits earned through prior learning assessment to non-major or free elective areas?

Is there a limit on the number of credits or courses you can earn through assessment of your prior learning?

Can you request credit for an advanced level of a subject area if you have not received credit for the basic or introductory level?[4]

Is there a limit on the number of credits or courses you can earn through an assessment of your prior learning?[5]

Let's see how some of the people in the case histories managed to equate their learnings to college courses.

Joan B.'s learnings were relatively easy to state in college course terms because most of the ones she wanted to use in her degree program were traditional in nature. Her list looks like this:

Art
   Introduction to Art History (based on formal training at the art museum and years of learning through museum attendance): 6 credits
   Egyptian Art and Culture (acquired from independent study for research paper): 3 credits
   Elementary Film Making (experiential learning while making film about "Artists in the City"): 3 credits

Communications
   Public Speaking (based on learning gained from lecturing at the museum): 2 credits

Social Work
   Substance Abuse Counseling (from experience with alcoholic husband and through reading and involvement with Alcoholics Anonymous): 3 credits
   Group Therapy (from reading and experience with Alcoholics Anonymous): 3 credits

Total Request: 20 credits

---

[4] This question sometimes arises in professional fields where a person may know in depth a subject that is ordinarily taught at an advanced level but has not yet learned all of the basic material that is commonly thought of as prerequisite. Some schools have solved this by agreeing to award the advanced credit only after the introductory course has been satisfactorily completed or by retitling the assessed learning and recommending the subsequent completion of the basic course. Since this is usually a faculty issue, our advice is to go ahead and make the credit claim and, if it turns out to be a problem, let the faculty solve it.

[5] If there is a limit, and you have enough potential credits to exceed that limit, you will have to make decisions about which of your learnings are the most important in terms of fulfilling requirements for your degree or reflecting on your transcript what you think are your most significant accomplishments.

Scott A.'s learnings were somewhat more difficult to fit into categories that meshed with his local community college's courses. With the help of his assessment counselor, he realized that what he had learned as a stock boy in a grocery store, while useful to a youngster as a first work experience, was not comparable to what colleges teach and, moreover, had nothing to do with his current educational and career plans. Those learnings, although they were important at a particular time in his life, were eliminated from his assessment list.

Since Scott wants to go into a two-year degree program in forestry, many of the learnings from his years with the paper company are relevant. The head of the department agreed that the experience gained from his years of work in the field were equivalent to the program's requirement of a six-credit field placement, or "practicum," and could be assessed for credit as such, but in addition he is requesting credit for three courses in the forestry curriculum.

The director of the physical education department said that although the school does not currently give a course in fishing, she would be willing to consider Scott's expertise in that area as a substitute for the physical education requirement if his learnings could be validated through a performance evaluation by a faculty member.

According to the college catalog, the English department did not offer a course in the literature of the Bible, but the religion and philosophy department did, so Scott has placed his learnings under titles that will be submitted to that department. He understands that simply demonstrating his factual knowledge of the Old and New Testaments is not enough; he must also show that he understands them on the levels of literature, myth, metaphor, and history; as textual accretion; and as primary religious and philosophical sources for the Judeo-Christian tradition.

The art department agreed to consider Scott's furniture making as a "craft" for which they could possibly award credit, but the college had no category under which his skills at carpentry and wood-working could be assessed.

So far, **Scott's** list of potential learnings for his portfolio looks like this:

Forestry
Operation of and Maintenance of Heavy Machinery (bull dozer, tractor, log hauler, skidder, etc.): 3 credits
Field Logging Operations, a Practicum: 6 credits
The Ecology of Forest Maintenance: 3 credits
The Technology of Papermaking: 3 credits

Physical Education
Fishing as a Sport: 1 credit

Religion and Philosophy
The Literature of the Old and New Testaments: 3 credits
Leadership Techniques for Bible Study: 2 credits

Arts and Crafts
Furniture Design, Making and Refinishing: 6 credits

Total Request: 27 Credits

Dorene's list:

Computer Science
Basic Computer Literacy: 3 credits
Office Technologies: 9 credits

Labor Relations
History of Labor Relations in the U.S.: 2 credits
Labor Negotiations and Arbitration: 2 credits

Modern Languages
Beginning and Intermediate Spanish: 6 credits
Latin American Literature and Culture: 2 credits

Political Science
History and Analysis of the Puerto Rican Statehood Movement: 3 credits

Total Request: 27 credits

Anna's list:

Psychology
Basic Child Psychology: 3 credits
Early Childhood Growth and Development: 3 credits
Practicum in Child Care: 3 credits

Business
  Management of Non-profit Organizations: 3 credits
  Personnel Management: 3 credits
  Public Relations: 3 credits
  Financial Management: 3 credits

Culinary Arts
  Basic Principles of Cooking and Baking: 6 credits
  Ethnic Cuisines: 3 credits

Total Request: 30 credits

Learning Components Method

"Learning components" is an educational phrase that refers to what you know and what you can do. It permits you to cluster your learning in the way you know it, rather than in the way college courses categorize and describe knowledge. Earlier we mentioned that experiential learning is sometimes "messy," that it doesn't fall into neat packages like college courses. Some institutions cope with this dilemma by encouraging individuals to "cluster" knowledge and skills by listing the specific skills, competencies, and accomplishments that reflect college-level learning.

Suppose, for example, that you know something about writing:

▲ you have worked in an office and know how to write business letters and memos;

▲ as part of your work with a volunteer agency, you regularly write press releases; and

▲ last year, you had a children's story published in a local magazine.

It is highly unlikely that you would find any one course in business, journalism, or creative writing to describe your knowledge and skill as a writer. Your knowledge may be broader or deeper, or contain a greater emphasis, than you will find in any particular college course description. In such a case you could cluster your learnings by listing your specific skills, competencies, and accomplishments. For example, you know how to:

▲ gather information;

▲ determine the important points;

▲ write simply and convincingly;

▲ tailor your writing to the audience and purpose;

▲ create imaginative characters; and

▲ handle narrative and point of view.

And you have considerable documentation to prove it! Your next step is to "translate" these learning components into some number of college credits. Upon consultation with the assessment counselor or a professor in the English department, you might be encouraged to request six credits for your writing competencies: three for the equivalent of a freshman writing course and three for an advanced writing course.

Using a College Catalog

One way to translate learning components into numbers of college credits is to "informally" use a written college course description (or a set of them, as in the college catalog). Although you may not be required to equate your knowledge to a specific course, the descriptions can be helpful. If you already have experience taking college courses and know in general what is expected in a standard three credit-hour course, you're one step ahead. For example, you took Principles of Accounting last year and earned three credit-hours. Now in your portfolio you are requesting credit in banking. You might assign a credit-hour value to your banking knowledge by recalling what was required to earn the credits in accounting. Perhaps you will only want to request two credits, or three or four, or even six, based on your recollection of the effort and content of a typical course.

College catalogs may also be used to compare your level of knowledge to that detailed in the course descriptions. As you read a particular description, ask yourself: do I *know* that, am I able to *do* that, is that what my *evidence* reflects? Estimate the percent of knowledge you think you have for each course that touches on your areas of expertise.

While course descriptions vary from very informative and detailed to quite sketchy, they are the most readily available sources of information. They can give you clues to what college faculty expect you to know in a particular field and are excellent tools that should be taken advantage of on your way to a degree.

Calculating College Credit

There is a second method of assigning a credit value to what you have learned that may be particularly useful if your knowledge was acquired through non-credit courses or workshops, such as may be sponsored through churches, community organizations, businesses and unions. The Carnegie Formula is a time ratio typically used by colleges in the United States to calculate college course credit.

A standard three credit-hour course requires students to spend 45 hours of class time and 90 hours of out-of-class work in order to receive credit. In other words, for every 15 hours of instruction and 30 hours of preparation, you earn one credit hour.

For example, suppose you attended a business management seminar sponsored by a major manufacturing company. The group met for six hours each week for five weeks, totalling 30 hours of time in the seminar. You estimate that you spent an additional 60 hours doing assignments and the required readings. With sufficient evidence to support your claim to credit (a course syllabus, list of readings and assignments, a document saying that you had indeed been enrolled in the course and passed it) you might want to request two credit hours. Alternatively, if the course is listed in the *ACE Guide*, most colleges will simply accept the guide's credit recommendation.

Help From Your College

In calculating your credit request, as in all the other decisions you will make in preparing for assessment, you can and should expect the college to help you, whether through providing a portfolio workshop or in making advice and assistance available to you through an assessment counselor.

▲ Organizing Your Portfolio

Well, you've assembled your list of learnings, related them to subjects taught in college, documented them, determined the amount of credit you will request, and written your essay or narrative. Now you are ready to put your portfolio together. It would be helpful if there were a single universal model portfolio to follow, but unfortunately there is no single model. Each institution has its own requirements, though some leave the final structure and organization of the portfolio up to the student.

The basic principle that should guide you in putting together your portfolio is this: *make it easy for the reader to understand.* Remember that your readers are busy people, college faculty and administrators, for whom reading your portfolio is only one of many, many tasks that they must accomplish in a typical day.

Your portfolio should be:

▲ *Selective.* Only those facts, learnings, documents, and data which are directly connected with your credit request should be included in the portfolio. Avoid redundancy.

▲ *Logically organized.* The plan or arrangement of the document should enable your readers to follow your thinking as they go from section to section. This means that you should keep your terminology consistent (don't call the same thing "business studies" in one section and "office procedures" in another) and keep things in the same order. If your learnings are listed chronologically in one place, don't switch to an alphabetical or order of importance listing in another place without clear explanation.

▲ *Coherent—the connections among the parts should be understandable.* Each section should be tied to the others with brief transitional statements or explanations if necessary, and the reader should never have to stop to question why you are bringing in an idea or information at a specific time.

▲ *Neat, grammatically correct, and clearly written.* The portfolio should look and read like a document worthy of a competent college student. Ideally it should be done through word processing for appearance and ease of revision. If you must settle for typing, that's fine, but edit carefully. Don't submit a handwritten document.

Despite the lack of a universal portfolio format, there are several elements that nearly all portfolio requirements have in common. The following elements give the portfolio coherence and "connectivity."

Cover Page

This should identify your institution and the name of the assessment program in which you are enrolled. It should also contain your name, address, and phone number, and include the date that you are submitting your portfolio. (See sample portfolio cover page in Exhibit 7-8.)

 Exhibit 7-8: Sample Portfolio Cover Page

PORTFOLIO FOR PRIOR LEARNING ASSESSMENT
submitted to
UNIONVILLE COLLEGE

ADULT ACCESS PROGRAM

by
DORENE DIAZ GARFIELD

November 6, 1997

2315 High Street
Starr City, Ark.
(717) 663-4768

Table of Contents

As in any book, the table of contents gives readers an overview of the organization of the portfolio and guides them to each of its sections. You may wish to do a first draft of a table of contents early on and use it as an outline of what you plan to include. Then, when you are ready to put the whole document together, revise the table of contents to correspond to any changes in your organization of material, and finally, add the correct page numbers.

Essay or Narrative

This part provides the assessor with a picture of who you are. As described earlier, the essay or narrative should show the relationship between your learning experiences and your college-level knowledge in the context of your life and educational goals. If, in the course of your work on this portfolio, you have also discovered some areas in which your present learning is inadequate and you intend to study further, this is information that your assessors should have. What is important is that you explain how your learnings relate to the further study you intend to pursue.

Learning Components, Competency Statements or Course Descriptions and Their Documentation in Each Learning Area Presented

This is the heart of most portfolios. It should identify each learning component or course for which you are seeking credit and provide the supporting documentation or evidence. It should also specify the number of credits you are seeking. For clarity's sake, this section should be preceded by a list of all the learning components, the documentation being submitted, and the number of credits requested.

Following this list (Exhibit 7-9) in Dorene's portfolio is a one-page competency statement for each area of learning (in the order in which they appear above), including the source of the learning and a detailed description of precisely what she has learned and/or can do, with the credit request on the bottom of the page and the documentation immediately following. Each item of documentation (transcripts, letters, certificates) has been marked in a way to connect it to the learning component which it addresses. Thus, Dorene has printed a large "C" in the upper right hand corner of the certificate for Union Course #410 so that the reader can easily identify the learning component to which it refers, an "F" on the letter from Dr. Haines, and so on. Although this attention to detail may seem unnecessary, it is critical if the readers are to be able to find their way around your portfolio, understand it, and make decisions about the merit of your credit request.

▲ **Exhibit 7-9:** List of Learning Components, Their Documentation, and Credits Requested (Example from Dorene G's Portfolio)

Learning Component	Documentation	Crs. Requested
A. Basic Computer Literacy	Letter from Employer	3 credits*
B. Office Technologies	PSI Certifying Exam Letter from Employer	9 credits*
C. History of Labor Relations in U.S.	Certificate of Partic. in Union Course #410 Facsimile of American Council on Education's credit recommendation for course #410	2 credits
D. Labor Negotiations and Arbitration	Letter from Union representative testifying to participation in process and level of competency	2 credits*
E. Beginning and Intermediate Spanish	CLEP test transcript	6 credits
F. History of the Puerto Rican Statehood Movement	Letter from Dr. A. Haines, Political Science Dept., Unionville College, testifying to level of competency	3 credits
G. South American Literature and Culture	Letter from Dr. K. Watts, Modern Languages Dept., Unionville College, testifying to competency	2 credits

TOTAL CREDIT REQUEST: 27 CREDITS

*To be applied to major in Business Studies

▲ Submitting Your Portfolio

Remember, **neatness counts**. For some of the people who read it, the portfolio will be all they will ever know of you, and if they must struggle with sloppy handwriting or poorly typed pages, they will associate their discomfort with the kind of person they suppose you to be. And if the manuscript is full of typos, errors, misspellings or incorrect grammar, they will have a difficult time divorcing their negative response to the language skills demonstrated in the portfolio from the other learnings you claim to have. Keep in mind that college-level knowledge, regardless of the subject area, assumes a basic competence in communication, writing in particular.

Revise and revise until the manuscript is as perfect as you can make it. Always have someone else check your work one last time for errors that you may have missed. If you are using word processing, be sure to take full advantage of spelling or grammar programs available.

Once you have assembled your portfolio and checked it one more time for completeness and accuracy, make a **duplicate copy** for your own records before submitting the original to the appropriate college office.[6] If some of your documentation (such as photographs, letters, or publications with your name on them) is valuable to you, ask if the school would be willing to accept the copies rather than the originals. For safety, these copies can be put in plastic envelopes designed for three-ring binders.

The day you hand in your portfolio you will probably experience an enormous sense of relief. When you submit evidence of your prior learning, you are also submitting a large piece of yourself— quite beyond the physical contents of your portfolio. This takes self-confidence, a high degree of motivation, and a willingness to take risks—surely the keys to success in any endeavor.

---

[6] The use of a three-ring binder, sized for standard-sized typing paper (8½ x 11), is convenient and enables you to make changes and rearrange pages as necessary. Standard dividers, sold in any stationery store, can be used to mark the divisions of the portfolio (essay, documentation, etc.), making it easier for the reader/assessor to locate information.

▲ Faculty Evaluation

Only one more hurdle remains: the actual assessment of your portfolio. In some colleges, the portfolio is assessed by a committee of faculty, or faculty and administrators. It becomes their task to read the entire document carefully; to weigh the evidence of learning; to make judgments as to whether that learning has the appropriate breadth, depth, and theoretical understanding to make it comparable to what you might have learned from similar college courses; to see if the documentation matches and supports the learning; to make certain that there is no overlap (for example, a request for credit for writing that looks similar to transcript credit for a freshman English course); to see how the learning fits into the student's degree program and overall education and career planning; and, finally, to weigh the credit request against the evidence of learning to see whether the request is reasonable.

Occasionally this process of assessment goes on without any further involvement on your part. More frequently, however, the assessment office will make an appointment with you to speak to faculty in some or all of your areas of learning, so that they may evaluate that learning in a face-to-face interview. This interview may be conducted as a casual conversation or as a more formal oral test, but in either case, its purpose is evaluative, that is, to see if your discussion of what you know matches up with what you have presented in your portfolio.

The faculty interview is not something to be dreaded. If yours is a strong portfolio presentation, the faculty person may simply want to confirm that you and your portfolio "match." Or the faculty person may wish to question you on something that was not quite clear, or may wish to find out whether what looked weak in your presentation arose from lack of knowledge or inadequate presentation of that knowledge.

Some students prepare for their faculty evaluations by reviewing a standard textbook that covers their experientially-gained knowledge. This is useful if you think you want to brush up on the vocabulary or "jargon" of a particular area, or if you want to refresh your memory of theory or specific facts.

In any case, you needn't dread the faculty evaluation. It will almost always be a benign procedure, fair, reasonable, and humanely conducted. Its purpose is to find out what you *do know*, not what you don't. In fact, the outcome of some faculty evaluations is a recommendation that the student's credit request should be *raised*.

▲ The Transcript

After your portfolio is assessed and the credit awards are recommended, you, the registrar, and sometimes the dean will be notified of the results.

The registrar is the college official who prepares students' transcripts—records of their progress and achievement in the college. It is the registrar's duty to record on your transcript the amount of credit you have earned through the portfolio process and to break it down into courses or learning components. The transcript becomes a document that follows you throughout life. If you wish to transfer credits to another college, or if you wish to apply for graduate school, or if you are applying for a job for which you need proof of credits or a degree, the transcript is the official document that you must produce.

A few weeks after the completion of assessment, you may wish to ask the registrar's office for a copy of your transcript so that you can check its accuracy and make certain that everything is in order.

You have done it. You have taken a lifetime of experience and turned it into a coherent account of the learnings produced by that experience. Whether you have earned six credits or 60, you have proved that you are an accomplished adult learner. You should feel a great sense of pride in your accomplishment, and should look to your future in college with renewed anticipation of reward and satisfaction.

In the next chapter, we will look at some of the issues you will face as you add being a student to your already crowded list of activities and responsibilities. And we will discuss some strategies for coping with the demands of going back to school.

C H A P T E R

8

Surviving and Thriving in College

I have but one lamp by which my feet are guided, and that is the lamp of experience.

Patrick Henry

Ok, this is it. You're going to be a student again. You've explored your career and life goals, you know what you want to do when you grow up, have identified the school that most closely meets your needs, have applied and been accepted, have talked to the assessment counselor and perhaps even registered for a prior learning assessment workshop, and have chosen the first course or courses you'll take. Suddenly you're getting nervous. You're wondering again if it's going to be too hard for you to manage, if you're going to be able to keep up with the others in your class, whether you have the ability to write a paper or take a test, or the courage to speak out when the professor asks for discussion.

Of course, lots of things would be different if you were 18 years old. Most of your friends would probably be starting college with you, and you could kid each other about being nervous and unsure. You'd be doing what everyone else would expect you to do at that age, and you wouldn't have to juggle a job and home responsibilities and maybe even children. But if you were 18 years old you wouldn't have all your valuable experience, and you wouldn't have such a clear sense of *why* you're taking this step and what you expect to get from it. You also probably wouldn't have the commitment that enables adult students to do so well when they return to the classroom.

If you were 18 years old, your mother might take you to the mall to buy you new shoes or a sweater and a nifty briefcase. Why don't you do it for yourself? Treat yourself! Celebrate! You're embarking on a great adventure, and it's going to be fun.

▲ Getting the Feel of the Campus

You'll be a lot more comfortable about going back to school if you don't wait until the first night of class to figure out in which building your course is meeting, how to get into the parking lot, or where the bookstore is. By now you should have talked to friends or co-workers who have gone to your college and read the college catalog, but some kinds of information about how a school "feels" are not readily available, either from people or printed information. To get a real sense of a school, you should probably take yourself on a campus tour. Talk to students as well as school officials, look over the library, the bookstore, the cafeterias or student hangouts, perhaps even sit in on a class or two. You may feel more comfortable if you go with your spouse or a friend. You may even find one or two people at work who will join you.

When you visit the campus, choose the time of day during which you will be attending class. Find each of the following locations, and *while you are there*, if possible, answer each of the following questions in your notebook.

1. Getting There

▲ How long did it take you to drive (or take the bus or train) from your home to the campus? Or from work to the campus? Did you travel in a time of heavy or light traffic? Is your class scheduled in a time of heavy or light traffic? How much time will you need to allow yourself to be sure that you get to class on time?

▲ Where did you park? Is there a lot reserved for students? Do you need a special parking pass or sticker to get into the lot? Where can you obtain such a pass? What will it cost?

▲ In what building is your class scheduled to be held? How far from the parking lot or bus stop is the building? How long will it take you to walk to your classroom building?

2. The Library

▲ Find the library. Go inside and look around. Find:

—the card catalog

—the "stacks" where books are shelved

—the section where current magazines and journals are kept

—the "reserve" book shelves where books that instructors have reserved for their students are kept

—the research section where dictionaries, encyclopedias, periodical indexes, and other research tools are available

—the audiovisual section, where you can view or listen to videotapes, films, records

—computers and typewriters for student use

▲ How is the library being used? What are people actually doing?

▲ Would you feel comfortable reading, studying, and doing research here?

▲ Ask one of the librarians what the hours of the library are, where you would find books in your field, and for how long a period books can be borrowed.

▲ Do you need a special library card to use the library, or is your college registration card sufficient?

▲ Is there an orientation tour of the library for new students? If so, sign up for it now.

▲ Has the old card catalog been replaced by a computerized system of information and retrieval? If so, ask a librarian for help in learning to use it.

Remember, the college library will be a critical resource for you, regardless of your field. The librarian's most important job is to help students, and you should take full advantage of that help in locating the printed and audiovisual materials you need, doing research, and utilizing the library's other services.

3. Other College Offices

▲ Where is the dean of students office, the admissions office, the registrar's office, the study skills center, the prior learning assessment office?

▲ What hours are each of these places open?

▲ Where is your instructor's office? Are regular office hours posted when he or she will be available?

4. In Classes and Between

▲ Observe the students emerging from class. Are they talking to each other? Do they seem enthusiastic about their studies?

▲ Peek into a few classrooms just as class is letting out. Are there students staying behind to talk with the professor? Does he or she seem friendly and helpful?

▲ Where do students go to hang out? Is there a cafeteria, a student lounge, a place where people seem to gather informally?

▲ How does the atmosphere of these places seem to you—friendly, reserved, boisterous and noisy?

▲ Are there other people of your age group? Gender? Ethnic background?

▲ Are most of the students dressed casually or do they seem dressed up? Is this a jeans and sneakers or a jacket and tie campus?

The more you can find out about the campus before you start class, the more relaxed you will be. The campus tour is a great way to prepare yourself for your new adventure.

▲ Managing Your Time

If you asked most working adults what is most precious to them (after their friends and family), they would probably say time. None of us seem ever to have enough time to do our paid jobs responsibly, take care of our families and homes, pay attention to our health and grooming needs, engage in community and social activities, and still go out to a ball game, play poker, read the newspaper or just "veg out." Now you're thinking about going back to school, and you're wondering how you're going to fit it all in.

First, let's look at how much time school is actually likely to take. There's the class time, of course—roughly three hours per week if you're taking a three-credit course. And then the two hours of reading and study that are theoretically needed to support each hour of classroom time—which for a three-credit course adds up to nine hours per week. (That number could be lower at some points in the semester, but could increase around exam time or when papers are due.)

But wait—that's not all. What about commuting time to and from the campus? And incidental time, like that spent seeing a counselor or tracking down your records in the registrar's office, having an appointment with your professor, working on your assessment portfolio, or just sitting down over coffee to talk to the guy who sits next to you in chemistry? Conservatively speaking, you should figure that going back to school for just one course will probably cost you at least an additional 12 to 16 hours of your time per week. Where's it going to come from?

There are many time management systems, but one of the simplest begins with constructing your own pie chart, finding out how you're currently spending your time so that you can begin to think about reallocating it.

Look at the four circles in exercise 8-1. Each is divided into 24 hours—and you can't have more than that no matter how clever you are. Think about that 24 hours. How much sleep must you have in order to function well? Six hours? Seven? Eight? And how much time do you work at your job per day? Eight hours? Plus commuting? What about taking care of your home, your children, the dog? Preparing and eating meals? Getting dressed? Calling your friends and relatives? Watching television?

If you asked most working adults what is most precious to them (after their family and friends), they would probably say time. Now you're thinking about going back to school, and you're wondering how you're going to fit it all in!

▼ Exercise 8-1: The Pie Chart System of Time Management

How I'm Managing My Time Now

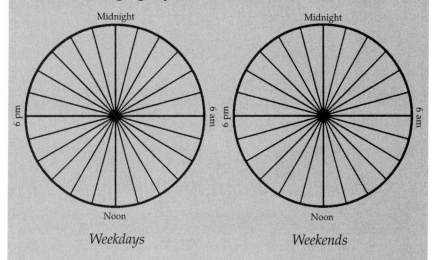

Weekdays

Weekends

How I'll Manage My Time When I'm In School

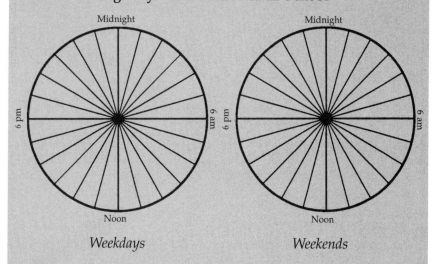

Weekdays

Weekends

Fill in the top left circle of exercise 8-1 with an approximation of how you are presently spending your allotted 24 hours during weekdays. And then fill in the top right circle for your weekends—good news, you may be able to pick up a few unscheduled hours on the weekends.

If you're like most of us, your first reaction to filling out the pie chart is likely to be that you don't even have time to do the things you're doing now; how can you take on going to school? Well, tens of thousands of adults are already doing it, but there's a cost. You have to be willing to look closely at how you're spending your time now to decide which activities are your real priorities and which could be dropped or turned over to someone else.

The "average" person uses his or her time in this way: sleep, 33 percent; work, 40 percent; maintenance, 15 percent (dressing, cooking, cleaning, exercising, etc.); free time, 12 percent (depends on family responsibilities).

What is "free" time? It's what's left over after sleep, work, and maintenance. It's the approximately 2.88 hours a day that you have to do everything else, whether playing with your kids, or having a beer with the gang, or listening to your favorite rock group.

So, in turning to the third and fourth pie charts—your projection of how you will allot your time to accommodate to going back to school—you have to make some hard decisions. This brings us to the classic time management system.

Classic Time Management System

All time management plans are based on a simple system of prioritizing tasks into three categories:

A. Very important/must do
B. Maintenance—get them done or they pile up
C. Need doing but can wait

Which tasks do you think are most popular? You guessed it—"C" tasks: groom the dog, read the sports page, call Aunt Leah in Chicago, watch reruns of "Seinfeld". . . Where did the time go?

"C" tasks are fun, low pressure and satisfying to cross off the list. "A" tasks are difficult, important, pressured, and carry the risk of failure. The first step is knowing the difference between A, B, and C tasks. Get in the habit of sorting out jobs on a daily and weekly basis using this system, and then get the A's and as many of the B's out of the way as you can.

"Wait a minute!" you're yelling. "I've only got the weekends and about three extra hours a day to do everything!" You're right, and that's why managing your time is a critical issue. You will probably have to give up some of your leisure activities for a while, and you may end up "buying time" from other people—having someone type your papers, the neighborhood youngster mow your lawn, or your kids take over feeding and grooming the cat.

Exercise 8-2 will help you get started.

▼ **Exercise 8-2:** Prioritizing Tasks

1. List 20 non-job activities that you perform in the course of an average month—anything from weeding and feeding the vegetable garden to having your mother-in-law to dinner to taking the Cub Scouts to the planetarium. Don't forget the obvious ones like paying bills, doing the laundry, driving Johnny to his karate lessons, and meeting your friends for a movie and beer on Friday nights.

2. Now prioritize these 20 activities as A, B or C.

3. Take a good hard look at your A's. Remember, A's are must dos. You must make certain that bills are paid, the family doesn't starve, the leak in the plumbing is fixed. But must you actually do all of these? Can you spend less time on them? Can you pay someone else to do them or get a friend or relative to help you out?

4. Look at your B's and C's. Which can you cut off the list? Which can you postpone or do less often? Which could someone else take over? Does your mother-in-law have to come to dinner every week? Maybe she'd enjoy going out for fast food with your spouse and kids occasionally while you're at school.

5. Look back over your whole list. How many of the 20 activities have you been able to eliminate? How much time have you saved?

▲

Although there are many time management techniques that you may want to learn about, this simple prioritizing method is a good basic tool for getting control of your time. Besides, it's very satisfying to have listed your A's, B's and C's so that you can have the pleasure of crossing them off as you go.

Energy Cycles

Next, figure out your own personal energy cycle. Some individuals have always been early risers, some night owls. Do you wake up at 5 a.m. whistling "Chariots of Fire?" Or are you the type that never misses Jay Leno? When are you most energetic and alert? Use that "prime time" for A tasks and save the B's and C's for times when you are less alert.

Until you get used to studying, taking notes, going to the library, and other new tasks, the whole business will probably take a greater amount of time than when these things are routine. So start out easy and plan ahead. And try to use your high energy times for your most demanding school work.

Beware the Time Vampires

Time can be stolen away if you're not careful. You won't want to live your entire life in such a careful way, but while you are in school you will need to be stingy about your time. For instance:

Make an agreement with your housemates about your study time, follow the agreement yourself and beware of repeat offenders. If your son always chooses your study time to ask for help with homework, sit down and have a little talk about why you are going to school and what it means for the family.

Stay off the phone. There is no law that you have to answer a telephone. They will call back if it's important. If someone else answers the phone, saying "I can't talk now, I'm studying," ought to do it.

Relax. You have probably established some standards in your life that come out of having enough time to enjoy high standards. Folded sheets in the cupboard, a well waxed car or a very tidy lawn are all great when you've got the time. You may temporarily have to slack off on some of these time-consuming activities to accomplish your goal.

Try to strike a balance between indulging yourself in all the partying, television, and baseball you've always enjoyed and denying yourself all pleasurable activities. You don't have to become a self-denying hermit for the next few years, but you probably will have to give up some activities you'll miss.

Clearly, going to school requires that you organize your life better than ever before. You will still feel pressured by such a full schedule, but you can manage if you are thoughtful about how you use your time and resources. You will probably have to give up some fun activities, but keep reminding yourself that you're not giving them up forever, and that you're gaining something very important: learning that will empower you and enable you to grow and make important career and personal changes in your life.

Talk openly with your family about this issue. You may be surprised by their willingness to help you tackle this problem.

▲ Creating a Support System

This is a time in your life when you're going to need to **shore up your support system**. What is a support system? It's the cluster of people in your life that you can count on. The people at work, at home and in your social life who are there when you need them, who will listen to your troubles, who can make you feel good about yourself, who will pitch in and help in an emergency.

Survey your own support system. Think about who you rely on. Who you wish you could rely on. Who disappoints you more times than helps you. Completing exercise 8-3 should help.

▼ **Exercise 8-3:** Surveying Your Support System

List the important people in your life under these categories:

Rooters. These are the people who are excited about your new plan. They will encourage you and give you emotional support.

_____

_____

_____

Constants. These are the people who like you just the way you are and feel a little nervous about how you may change if you go back to school. They're not against the idea, but they don't like the idea of changes, period.

_____

_____

_____

Resources. These are the people at work and in school, in the library, wherever, who have the information and services that can make it easier for you.

_____

_____

_____

Challengers. These are the people you look up to for guidance and inspiration. They are your advisors, mentors and role models. They may be people who have already done what you want to do and they can give you good advice as well as encouragement.

_____

_____

_____

Toxics. These are people who put you down and sabotage your efforts because of their own problems. They are people who drain your energy and make you feel uncertain.

_____

_____

_____

I hope your list of rooters is longer than your toxics! Don't be surprised if you've listed some of the people in your family in more than one category, including a mix of positives and negatives. Your going to school will definitely affect them, and it is a good idea to keep communication open as you go along.

For example, a husband may be very proud of his wife's going back to school (rooter), but still resent the fact that she's gone two nights a week (toxic). Your Aunt Sarah may offer to help you out by doing the food shopping for you on weekends (resource), but you have the feeling that deep down she thinks you're just complicating your life unnecessarily (constant).

The challenge is to find ways to move those closest to you into positive roles, to turn potential constants and toxics into rooters, resources, and challengers. You might want to spend considerable time making certain that your children understand why you're going to school and what positive consequences it will have for all of you as a family when you achieve your goal. If they can understand that you will be in line for a better job at higher pay which will make life easier for everyone, or if they can be made to see that your commitment to learning will bring you closer to them while they are also learning in school, or if they are secure in knowing that less time together doesn't mean less love, then they will be better able to tolerate your absences, the lack of home baked desserts, the many inconveniences of having a parent who is less available to them than before.

It's also a good idea to include your spouse or best friend in some of your new interests and activities when you're going to school. Discuss a great idea you got from your political science course, ask your friend to accompany you to an open lecture on campus, show your spouse how a new accounting procedure might work on the family budget, invite a classmate home to meet your nearest and dearest.

Of course, your support system, no matter how strong, works best if it starts with you. Your confidence that you can make it, your pride in being a lifelong learner, your commitment to what you are doing, form the bedrock of your success. Be your own best rooter. Your family has a right to know what they are getting into, and so do you. As part of their preparation for going to school, some adults have negotiated contracts with their families or housemates, spelling out each person's duties, privileges and trade-offs.

Strategies for Negotiating a Contract _____

For some families, a formal, written contract is a good way of making sure that everyone involved understands what kinds of support you will need in going back to school and what kinds of trade-offs there will be. Sitting down to talk this out with parents, spouses, children, or the friends with whom you live, and then spelling out on paper the agreements reached, can be a great way of getting these issues out in the open before they can cause hurt feelings or resentment.

Keep in mind that contracts are a two-way street. Every contract means compromise on both sides. Your family members have a right to their own reasonable demands. If, for example, you play cards two weekday nights and now plan to attend college the other two, of course your family will protest your absence four nights in a row each week. Your understanding response to their concerns (and your willingness to make a few deals) is the best strategy you've got.

Your contract might include some of the following issues:

A. The Quiet Clause: No music will be played in the house from 8 to 11 p.m. on Tuesday or Wednesday. In return, Bob and Karen will be allowed to eat dinner in front of the TV on those nights.

B. The Card Game Clause: Instead of playing cards two evenings a week (or going to ball games or shopping or visiting friends), Frank will now attend school two evenings a week and play cards once every other week.

C. The Burger King Clause: Paul will be responsible for feeding the kids on the evenings Mary is in school. He is allowed to take them to Burger King as often as he wishes.

Important Note: Only negotiate contract clauses that you are really prepared to live with, and once you've got the contract, keep to it. Subsequent extra nights out or complaints about the lack of nutritional value in fast foods are against the rules.

Our friend **Max** (see profiles, chapter 2) has a contract with his girl friend that she will baby sit for him three nights a week while he's in class and will type his papers. In return, he has offered to take over the maintenance of her car (a job she hates) and will keep one night a week free so that they can attend dance recitals and go to the theatre (her special interests, which Max has always been reluctant to accommodate). **Anna**, who is back in school now, has contracted with her youngest son (the only one still at home) to increase his allowance in return for his taking over the family shopping and laundry. Her husband has agreed to clean the house on Saturdays, and they have all agreed that they will forego Anna's superb cooking a few nights a week and go out for inexpensive dinners. Although the whole family is delighted that Anna is finally doing something for herself, they tease her about becoming an "egghead."

Know Your Family

Your in-depth knowledge of your own family's personalities and needs may prove to be the most important factor in getting through the next few years with relationships not only intact but even strengthened. If your wife hates clutter on the kitchen table, set up a card table in the bedroom for studying. If your husband hates not watching evening TV, plan to study in the library a few times a week. If your kids are proud that Mommy or Daddy is going to school, too, do your homework together from time to time.

▲ Money Matters

If you're like most adults, you've probably already begun to think about what college will cost, and you've found out that per course or per credit charges vary widely. Although state and locally supported schools may be much less expensive than private colleges and universities, you should not automatically make your decision based on cost. While a community college that charges $50 per credit may seem a real bargain when compared to a college that charges $200 per credit, you owe it to yourself to make certain that your first priority is to choose the school that offers the programs or courses you need. (See chapter 4.) Sometimes the more expensive schools may become affordable through their special scholarships or through a particularly generous financial aid package.

If you're lucky, you work for a company or belong to a union that has education benefits that will cover some or all of the tuition. Some companies advertise their tuition benefits widely; others don't publicize them. Talk to your own company's benefits person to find out what their policy is and if you qualify. Even if you can't get help from your employer, however, there are a number of sources of financial aid that may be available to you. In recent years, with the increasing numbers of adults going back to school, some programs have begun to include part-time students as eligible for aid.

The major kinds of financial aid include:

Grants—These may be from federal, state or college sources, and may vary widely in amount, but typically they are tied to financial need and dependent upon your being enrolled in an eligible institution and making satisfactory progress in your classes.

Loans—The sources and amounts of loan programs may vary from year to year and program to program, but in general they are made by state and federal governments or by local lending institutions and colleges. They are usually at an interest rate somewhat below that charged for conventional loans.

Scholarships—These vary widely from school to school, and from one geographic area to another, and may be sponsored by the college or by outside groups with an interest in education. They may cover all or part of tuition costs, and may also include stipends for books or housing. Scholarships may be granted on the basis of merit or grade-point average or because you belong to a special group (women, minorities, children of people in certain professions, etc.) for which money has been set aside.

College Work-Study—This is a program jointly sponsored by the college and federal government in which the student is paid for working for the college for a given number of hours per month.

As you can see, financial aid is a complicated subject which varies from one school to another and also changes from year to year as federal and state governments develop new programs to help people go to college. Moreover, students are not necessarily limited to just one kind of tuition aid. It is frequently possible to put together a package of loans and grants, or loans and scholarships, depending on the student's financial needs and full or part-time, graduate or undergraduate status.

Don't despair. *Help is available.* Every college has a **financial aids officer** whose responsibility it is to give you the information you need about the kinds of aid available to you and to assist you in making applications. Sometimes you will find that the more expensive colleges turn out to be affordable because of the greater variety of financial aids packages they can put together.

While educational benefits may pay for the most expensive part of going to school, tuition and fees, there will be additional costs like books, school supplies, transportation, parking, snacks, etc. Depending upon the course or program in which you are enrolled, books may represent a substantial investment, particularly in some of the technical or professional fields. And many colleges recommend that every student have a personal computer.

Even without the major cost of a computer, the beginning of each term may require up to $200 in cash. Can you budget ahead for that? It may be useful for you to try to calculate the true cost of returning to school using the items in exercise 8-4 as your guide:

▼ **Exercise 8-4:** Calculating the Cost of School

Tuition* _____

Books** _____

Supplies
(possibly including a PC) _____

Fees* _____

Household Help _____

Quick Foods _____

Transportation _____

Child Care _____

Other _____

TOTAL _____

*These may be covered by educational benefits.
**Most college bookstores put out the texts ordered for each course a few weeks before class starts. You can estimate the cost of books by finding the section where your course's books are on display and simply adding up the prices. (You could also buy the books early and get a head start on your reading.)

▲

▲ Developing Good Study Habits

Having a Place to Study

Dorene finds it difficult to study in her apartment with her room-mate yakking on the phone or listening to music or wanting to talk to her. She goes to the college library after work three nights per week and on Saturdays goes to her local community library for a few hours. She has gotten to know the librarians at both places, and they help her find the information and books she needs. The college library has individual "carrels," small desks where she can read and take notes and leave her books and papers while she is at the card catalog or out for a snack, and she finds that when she is working at her carrel, her concentration is so intense she loses track of time.

Joan has converted a large closet in her home into a study. She fitted her grandmother's small antique desk into the space, hung her favorite Picasso print above it, installed a strong overhead light, and built open book/storage shelves along one wall, with a pull out shelf for her laptop computer. Her sons know that when she is in her "study" they are not to call her to the phone or bother her for anything less than a full scale emergency.

Max can concentrate anywhere, anytime. Because he doesn't want his children to feel excluded by his studying, he has set up regular hours when he and they sit around the kitchen table doing their "homework." The rule is that he and the kids must be quiet for 45 minutes of every hour, but then can spend 15 minutes talking, during which time he can help them with their problems and explain what he is doing. They also share jokes and stories, and tease and encourage each other during these 15 minute breaks.

You will need a place to study and store your school books and materials, a place that is comfortable and private (unless you're like Max), that has good lighting and a minimum of distracting clutter. It can be a card table in a corner of the bedroom or a mahogany desk in the den, but everyone else in the house has to recognize that it's yours and keep hands off.

There is no perfect way to study for everyone. You need to take account of your own preferences and timetable. Some people, if they have a lot of reading to do, stretch out in bed to do it. Other people

You will need a place to study and store your materials, a place that is comfortable and private, that has good lighting and a minimum of distracting clutter.

find that if they lie down they go to sleep, so they do their reading at a desk.

Make a study schedule for yourself and share it with the people with whom you live. Post it on the door or the refrigerator to generate support and sympathy.

Here are a few general hints most students find helpful:

1. Always (or as much as possible) study in the same place. It seems to condition your brain in a positive way so that when you arrive at your study area, you concentrate more quickly. You are also less likely to lose things if you have one place to work.

2. Take regular "breaks" from reading. A walk to the kitchen sink for a glass of water will pep you up for another 10 pages. While you're on your break, talk out loud to yourself about what you've just read. If you can explain it to yourself you have a better chance of remembering it.

3. Study the hard stuff while you have the most energy. If math is tough for you, work on it first and then read your psychology assignment or *Moby Dick*. Avoid the temptation to do what you like first.

4. Don't forget the library. Not only is the library designed for study with good lighting, quiet areas, and comfortable study furniture, but the librarian can help you find materials you need. In addition, in some courses the professor will have put some required reading books and journals on "reserve," which means that you will have to spend time in the library reading them.

For a helpful list of tips for "efficient study," see appendix I.

Creating a Study Plan

You may be taking a typical three hour English class, a standard requirement for any degree. Including reading and writing compositions, you will probably need to study five or six hours a week. Make a plan showing where and when you will study, including time at the library for research and time for typing the weekly two to three page compositions required for the class.

Most professors hand out a "syllabus" the first week of class. A syllabus usually includes a list of the textbooks or other materials required for the course, class-by-class or week-by-week reading assignments, and dates for papers due and exams. Use your class syllabus to plot your course on a calendar so that you'll know exactly how much reading you have to do each week, when you're going to need extra time to complete written work, and when you'll be busy studying for mid-semester or final exams.

MY STUDY PLAN

class hours   _____

study hours   _____

library visits   _____

study location   _____

typewriter/computer location   _____

Study Skills

Study skills are those competencies that enable you to learn more easily, retain that learning, and demonstrate it through oral and written tests and compositions. They include:

reading efficiently
remembering material
understanding material
taking notes
using the library
writing papers
doing math problems
preparing for tests
taking tests

You're not born with study skills. You learn them. Most students, of all ages, come to school with weak study skills in some areas, but these weaker skills can be strengthened through books and programs, tutoring and practice. Many schools even offer a one-credit course in study skills, which might be worth your time and effort if you suspect you need help.

There is no perfect way to study for everyone. You need to take account of your own preferences and timetable.

Reinforcing Your Study Skills

Although adults frequently worry that they may have forgotten how to study or will have a hard time competing with younger students, colleges' experience with adult students has demonstrated that adults are usually better students because they are motivated and have defined goals. Research tells us that returning adult students, on the average, maintain better grades than younger students.

While at first you may feel slightly ill at ease if there are a lot of younger students in your classes, you will find that your lifelong learning experiences and mature goals actually give you the edge. While younger students are partying on a Friday night, older students are often in the library. Older students seem better able to pace themselves, to study throughout the semester rather than "cramming" at the last minute.

Still, you probably haven't spent a lot of time reading or memorizing over the past few years. Some of your skills, like composition or math, may be a little rusty. But then younger students also have trouble with basic skills sometimes. That's why all colleges have basic skills centers (or tutoring centers or remedial skills centers—the names vary) where help is available to improve your reading speed and comprehension, composition skills, test taking skills and basic math skills. Most centers offer assessment tests, sometimes called diagnostic tests, that give you an estimate of your current skills levels and how much help you may need. Experts can then assign you to specific learning programs designed to help you build your basic skills or can match you up with a tutor. Some basic skills programs are on computers and can be worked on at your own pace, concentrating exactly on those areas where you need the most help.

Basic skills services are free, and they work. Don't be shy about using them. They exist because there is a need for them, and they are designed to bring students "up to speed" as quickly as possible.[1]

---

[1] For a short, down-to-earth introduction to study skills, look at *Study is Hard Work* by William H. Armstrong (Boston: David R. Godine Publ., 1995).

Reading Efficiently

Reading efficiently is critical if you are to get the maximum information from your textbooks in minimum time. Think of the chapter titles in the textbook as a series of mental stepping stones which, if followed, will lead you to an understanding of the subject of that text. Paying attention to how each chapter is arranged (through headings and subheadings, time sequence, in ascending or descending levels of importance, etc.) is a good way of figuring out which information is critical for you to remember. Underlining the critical information will help you when it comes time to study for an exam.

If there are study questions at the end of each chapter, try to answer them. If you can't, go back and reread the chapter. Make use of illustrations, graphs, bibliographies, and footnotes to clarify what you're studying or to lead you to other resources.

Taking Notes

Taking good notes in class is critical. You don't need to copy every word the instructor says; you can capture the important information. Most instructors lecture from an outline which helps make what they are saying clear to a careful listener. If the instructor says there are three main points, or four people, or five reasons for something, make sure you get them all down. They will likely reappear on the next test. If you miss something, don't worry. You can check it out with another student, or even better, use it as a reason to make an appointment to talk to the instructor. It's always a good idea to get to know the faculty and for them to get to know you. If you know ahead of time that you're going to miss a class, you might ask another student to tape it for you.

Using the Library

If it's been years since you've used a library, you'll find it's changed a lot. Most libraries today are "on-line." The old rows of wooden drawers that held the card catalog have given way to computer terminals on which you can call up the books you want by author, title, or subject. There are new, computerized bibliographies, indexes and other materials that will enable you to do research more efficiently than in the past, and audiovisual materials of a variety and sophistication never dreamed of when you were last in school.

Don't worry about feeling at sea in this brave new world. Ask for help! That's why there are librarians, and they will be delighted to introduce you to the electronic wonders of today's libraries. If you know what information you need, they can tell you how to find it in the simplest way possible, and within a short time you'll be having a lot of fun finding your own way.

▲ Troubleshooting

No matter how well you have planned your going back to school, glitches can occur. As a popular philosopher puts it, bad things *can* happen to good people. A college computer can fail so that you get to a class for which you have registered and your name isn't on the instructor's list. A course you really want may be cancelled for insufficient registration or changed to a time that is inconvenient. You can find yourself in a class that seems way above your head. The bookstore may have run out of copies of the chemistry text. You may get back your first history paper, on which you worked for hours and hours, and there's a big fat "D" in the upper right hand corner. You don't like your advisor. You need a parking sticker and don't know where to go.

Well, the first thing to remember is "Don't panic." The second thing is, "You aren't the first one who's ever had this problem. And there are always solutions."

Think of yourself as a competent adult with the ability to speak up for yourself. Think of yourself also as a consumer. You are paying a lot of money for an education. You have a right to make certain demands on the college.

You won't be the first or last one to challenge a *%$#*&! computer (or the human being who probably made the error), or to go to the registrar's office to change your schedule, or to make an appointment with an instructor to find out why he gave you a low grade, or to ask for help in understanding some knotty material. In fact, the more assertive you are about getting the information and help you need, the more people you will get to know on campus and the more respect you will have from others (and yourself). So ask questions. Track down the officials or faculty who can take positive action. Don't take no for an answer without finding out why. Look for alternatives. And above all, keep your sense of humor.

No matter how busy you are, try to make time to talk to your fellow students and professors, in and out of class. A college education can and should be far more than a series of classes taken, exams passed, credits accumulated and degrees awarded. Ideally, it is a series of learning experiences both in and out of the classroom that draw you into a learning society or learning culture.

▲ Not All of a College Education Occurs in the Classroom

OK. You have to race home after work to walk the dog, and then you hurry to the campus, arriving just in time for your class. After class you have to get back to relieve the baby sitter, so you pass up the chance to ask the professor why he thinks Saul Bellow is a better writer than Stephen King, and you say no thanks to the couple sitting behind you who asked if you wanted to go out for a beer. You may have blown your chance to enrich your education.

A college education can and should be far more than a series of classes taken, exams passed, credits accumulated, and degrees awarded. A college education, ideally, is a series of learning experiences, both in and out of the classroom, that draw you into a learning society or learning culture. Going to college should give you access to new friends, men and women who care about learning and who share it gladly. It should challenge your ideas, enlarge your horizons, make you think about people, art, politics, religion, and the environment in new ways.

No matter how busy you are, try to make time to talk to your fellow students and professors, in and out of class; read the college newspaper to find out what's going on; attend special lectures or meetings on subjects that interest you. If there's an adult student organization on campus, join it. These extracurricular activities can open up whole new worlds for you and make the experience of going back to school more intellectually and personally stimulating than you ever dreamed.

APPENDIX

A

Ten Standards for Quality Assurance in Assessing Learning for Credit*

▲ Academic Standards

1. Credit should be awarded only for learning and not for experience.

2. College credit should be awarded only for college-level learning.

3. Credit should be awarded only for learning that has a balance, appropriate to the subject, between theory and practical application.

4. The determination of competence levels and of credit awards must be made by academic experts in the appropriate subject matter.

5. Credit should be appropriate to the academic context in which it is accepted.

---

*Urban Whitaker, *Assessing Learning: Standards, Principles, & Procedures.* Philadelphia: CAEL, 1989.

▲ Administrative Standards

6. Credit awards and their transcript entries should be monitored to avoid giving credit twice for the same learning.

7. Policies and procedures applied to assessment, including provision for appeal, should be fully disclosed and prominently available.

8. Fees charged for assessment should be based on the services performed in the process and not determined by the amount of credit awarded.

9. All personnel involved in the assessment of learning should receive adequate training for the functions they perform, and there should be provision for their continued professional development.

10. Assessment programs should be regularly monitored, reviewed, evaluated, and revised as needed to reflect changes in the needs being served and in the state of the assessment arts.

B

Useful Books for Career Planning

Asher, Donald. *The Foolproof Job-Search Workbook.* Berkeley, CA: Ten Speed Press, 1995.
> Information on the hidden job market, networking, resumé writing.

Barkley, Nella and Eric Sandburg. *Taking Charge of Your Career.* New York: Workman Publications, 1995.

Bernstein, Alan B. and Nicholas R. Schaffzin. *The Princeton Review Guide to Your Career.* New York: Random House, 1996.
> Includes information on job requirements, salary ranges, a self-assessment profile to help you identify your potential.

Bolles, Richard N. *The Three Boxes of Life: An Introduction to Life/Work Planning.* Berkeley, CA: Ten Speed Press, 1990.

Bolles, Richard N. *The 1997 What Color is Your Parachute? A Practical Manual for Job-Hunters and Career-Changers*. Berkeley, CA: Ten Speed Press, 1996.
  This deservedly popular book covers self-assessment, career planning, and job hunting.

Dorio, Marc. *The Complete Idiot's Guide to Getting the Job You Want*. New York: Alpha Books, 1995.

Holland, John L. *Making Vocational Choices: A Theory of Vocational Personalities and Work Environments*. Englewood Cliffs, NJ: Prentice-Hall, 1985.

Holland, John L. *The Self-Directed Search: A Guide to Educational and Vocational Planning*. Odessa, FL: Psychological Assessment Resources, Inc., 1985.
  A short booklet with questions that help you explore your feelings and attitudes about different kinds of occupations. It is an excellent tool for helping people make basic career decisions.

Occupational Outlook Handbook. U.S. Department of Labor, Bureau of Labor Statistics, 1990.
  For each of the hundreds of occupations listed in this book, there is information on the nature of the work, working conditions, employment (numbers, types, locations), training needed, other qualifications, advancement, job outlook, earnings, and related occupations. (See your library or order from Superintendent of Documents, U.S. Government Printing Office, Washington, D.C. 20402.)

Pogrebin, L. C. *Getting Yours: How to Make the System Work for the Working Woman*. New York: McKay, 1975.

Rockcastle, Madeline T., ed. *Where to Start: An Annotated Career-planning Bibliography*. Career Center, Cornell University: Peterson's Guides. (Updated periodically)

Yate, Martin. *Knock 'Em Dead*. Holbrook, Mass.: Adams Publ., 1996.
  Helpful sections on job interviews, electronic job searches.

APPENDIX C

General Skills List

Management Skills	Communications Skills	Research Skills
Planning	Reasoning	Recognizing problems
Organizing	Organizing	Interviewing
Scheduling	Defining	Developing questions
Assigning/ delegating	Writing	Synthesizing
Directing	Listening	Writing
Hiring	Explaining	Diagnosing
Measuring production	Interpreting ideas	Collecting data
Setting standards	Reading	Extrapolating
Work under stress	Handle precision work	Reviewing
Work with people	Work with committees	Work without direction
Travel frequently	Public speaking	Work very long hours
Work as a team member	Correct English usage	

Management Skills	Communications Skills	Research Skills
Personnel practices	Operate	Work on long-term
Time management	communication	projects
Negotiating	systems	Statistics
strategies	Good sense of time	Algebra
		Research design

Financial Skills	Manual Skills	Service Skills
Calculating	Operating	Counseling
Projecting	Monitoring	Guiding
Budgeting	Controlling	Leading
Recognize	Setting-up	Listening
problems	Driving	Coordinating
Solve problems	Cutting	Work under stress
Finger dexterity	Work independently	Work on weekends
Orderly thinking	Knowledge of tools	Work night shifts
Accounting	Safety rules	Knowledge of a
procedures	Basic mechanics	subject
Data processing	Basic plumbing	Human behavior
Operate business	Electronic principles	principles
machines		Community
Financial concepts		resources
Investment principles		Agencies' policies

Clerical Skills	Technical Skills	Public Relations Skills
Examining	Financial	Planning
Evaluating	Evaluating date	Conducting
Filing	Calculating	Maintaining
Developing	Adjusting controls	favorable image
methods	Aligning fixture	Informing the
Improving	Following	public
Recording	specifications	Consulting
Computating	Observing	Write news
Recommending	indicators	releases
Work as a team	Verifying	Researching
member	Drafting	Representing
Work in office	Designing	Work with people
Follow directions	Work in an office/	Work under stress
Do routine office	outdoors	Work very long
work	Work in small	hours
Basic clerical skills	studios	Work odd hours
Bookkeeping	Odd hours	Negotiating
Data-entry	Economics	principles
operations	Investigation principles	Media process
	Balancing principles	Human relations

Agricultural Skills	Selling Skills	Maintenance Skills
Diagnosing malfunctions	Contracting	Repairing equipment
Repairing engines	Persuading	Maintaining equipment
Maintaining machinery	Reviewing products	Operating tools
Packing	Inspecting products	Dismantling
Replacing defective parts	Determining value	Removing parts
Woodworking	Informing buyers	Adjusting functional parts
Constructing buildings	Promoting sales	Lubricating/ cleaning parts
Hitching	Work outdoors/ indoors	Purchasing/ ordering parts
Work outdoors	Work with people	Climbing
Work in varied climate	Work under stress	Work indoors/ outdoors
Manual work	Work long hours	Lift heavy equipment
Do heavy work	Knowledge of products	Work as a team member
Operating basic machinery	Human relations	Basic mechanics
Safety rules	Financing	Electrical principles
Welding	Budgeting	Plumbing principles
Horticultural procedures		

D

Independent Learning Opportunities

Obtaining a college degree doesn't necessarily mean attending classes. There are a number of educational institutions at which you may work towards an associate, bachelor's or doctoral degree without setting foot in a classroom.

The following "independent learning" institutions offer programs for adults for whom attending a traditional college or university may be impossible. Each accepts out of state students and each has graduated hundreds of men and women whose degrees have led to personal and professional advancement. For further information, call or write to:

American Open University of New York
Institute of Technology
Building 66, Office 227
Central Islip, NY 11722
(516) 348-3000

Board of Governor's Universities (Governors State, Chicago State, Eastern Illinois, Northeastern Illinois and Western Illinois Universities) geared to the needs of adult learners and offering a variety of distance learning options. For more information call:

Western Illinois University, School of Extended and Continuing Education, (309) 298-1864

or

Governors State University, Center for Extended Learning and Communications Services
(708) 534-4087
http://govst.edu

Center for Distance Learning
Empire State College
2 Union Avenue
Saratoga Springs, NY 12866
(518) 587-2100
http://www.esc.edu

Ohio University External Student Program
309 Tupper Hall
Athens, OH 45701
(800) 444-2420

Regents College of the University of the State of New York
Cultural Education Center
Albany, NY 12230
(518) 474-3703

Thomas A. Edison State College
101 West State Street
Trenton, NJ 08625
(609) 984-1100

▲ Other Resources

KNOWLEDGE TV is a national cable network dedicated exclusively to educational programming. Through COLLEGE CONNECTIONS it delivers college-level classes for credit in conjunction with numerous fully-accredited colleges and universities. Its offerings include a course adapted from this book called *Earn College Credit for What You Know.*

Knowledge TV is available through local cable programming; satellite television; and VHS tapes.

To order a catalog or materials, call the Knowledge Store, (800) 940-6463. For information about college classes and degree programs, call College Connections at (800) 777-MIND.

E-mail: meu.edu
Website: www.jec.edu

▲ Printed Materials

Campus-Free College Degrees, 7th ed. Marcie Kisner Thorson. Holbrook, Mass.: Adams Media Corp., 1996.
> Thorson's book covers 150 accredited off-campus college degree programs and is available in most large book stores, or call (918) 622-2811.

The Adult Learner's Guide to Alternative and External Degree Programs. Dr. Eugene Sullivan.
> Order by mail: American Council on Education, One Dupont Circle, Suite # 250, Washington, D.C., 20036.

External Degrees in the Information Age: Legitimate Choices. Henry A. Spille, David W. Stewart, Eugene Sullivan. Phoenix, AZ: Oryx Press/American Council on Education, 1997.

How to Study Independently. Regents College (free). Call (518) 474-3703.

Innovative Graduate Programs Directory. Empire State College. Call (518) 587-2100 ext. 365.

Directory of Accredited Home Study Schools.
> A brochure of school names, subject areas, a description of each program and contact information. For a copy of the Directory call CAEL at (800) 327-2235.

E

Assessment Resources

▲ Testing Programs

Advanced Placement Program (APP)

Tests in 30 academic subjects, usually taken by high school seniors for advanced placement in college courses, but may be accepted by some colleges as part of prior learning assessment.

For further information, write to:

Advanced Placement Program
Educational Testing Service
Rosedale Road MS 50-D
Princeton, New Jersey 08540
Voice: (609) 771-7300
FAX: (609) 530-0482
E-mail: apexams@ets.org
Website: www.ets.org

ACT-PEP Regents College Examinations

Over 42 tests covering the following areas:

Nursing
Business
Arts and Sciences
Education

For further information, write to:

ACT Operations (85)
2201 N. Dodge Street
P.O. Box 168
Iowa City, IA 52243-0168
Voice: (319) 337-1363
FAX: (319) 337-1578

College Level Examination Program (CLEP)

The five *general exams* cover material taught in courses that most students take as requirements in the first two years of college.

English Composition, or English Composition with Essay
Humanities
Mathematics
Natural Sciences
Social Sciences and History

The over 30 *subject exams* cover material taught in undergraduate courses in history, political science, psychology, economics, sociology, foreign language, composition and literature, science, mathematics and business.

For further information, write to:

CLEP
P.O. Box 661
Princeton, NJ 08541-6601
Voice: (609) 771-7865
FAX: (609) 771-7681
E-mail: clep@ets.org
Website: http//w.collegeboard.org

DANTES Subject Standardized Tests (DSSTs)

DANTES Subject Standardized Tests are credit-by-examination tests similar to CLEP covering what would usually be taught in a semester-long college course. The DSST program includes over 30 test titles in physical science, social science, business, applied technology, humanities, and mathematics. For further information, write to:

DANTES Program Office
The Chauncey Group International
504 Carnegie Center
Princeton, NJ 08540
Voice: (609) 951-6264
FAX: (609) 951-6767

or

DANTES Program
Educational Testing Service
Princeton, New Jersey 08541-1001
Voice: (609) 771-7850
FAX: (609) 771-7845
E-mail: DANTES@Chauncey.com
Website: http:/www.Chauncey.com/gov/htm/dantest.html

Job Ready Level Assessment

The Job Ready Level Assessment Tests are designed to measure proficiency in a broad range of occupational/vocational areas through written and performance tests.

For further information contact:

National Occupational Competency Testing Institute (NOCTI)
500 N. Bronson Avenue
Big Rapids, Michigan 49307
Voice: (616) 796-4695
FAX: (616) 796-4699
Website: www.nocti.org

Other highly respected examination programs include

New York University Proficiency Testing in Foreign Languages
Foreign Language Program
NYU School of Continuing Education
2 University Place, Room 55
New York, NY 10003

Ohio University Examination Program
Lifelong Learning
309 Tupper Hall
Athens, Ohio 45701

Thomas A. Edison State College Examination Program
TECEP
Office of the Registrar
101 West State Street CN545
Trenton, New Jersey 08625

▲ Licenses and Certificates in Professional Areas

Many colleges and universities use a student's possession of professional licenses and certificates as a basis for awarding credit for prior learning. Many of these professional licenses and certificates, in turn, are based upon some combination of work experience, instruction, and examinations. Here is a *partial* listing of some widely recognized licenses and certificates.

Chartered Life Underwriter (CLU)

Chartered Property Casualty Underwriter (CPCU)

Certificate in Data Processing (CDP)

Certificate in Computer Programming (CCP)

Certified Professional Secretary (CPS)

Certified Public Accountant (CPA)

Chartered Financial Consultant (ChFC)

FAA Air Traffic Control Specialist

FAA Airline Transport Pilot

FAA Commercial Pilot Airplane License

FAA Commercial Pilot Rotocraft License

FAA Mechanic Certificate/Airframe and Power Plant Rating

FAA Multiengine Airplane

FAA Private Pilot Airplane License

FAA Private Pilot Rotocraft License

Registered Professional Reporter

Listing of other licenses, certificates and training programs that are credit-worthy may be found in:

American Council on Education. *The National Guide to Educational Credit for Training Programs.* New York: Macmillan, 1986.

▲ Evaluated Programs

NOTE: Both of the following guides should be available in libraries or in college assessment counselors' offices.

Guide for the Program on Non-Collegiate Sponsored Instruction. (PONSI). Sponsored by the American Council on Education (ACE). PONSI evaluations have been done on several hundred corporate, union and government training programs.

A Guide to the Evaluation of Educational Experiences in the Armed Services. American Council on Education (ACE).
Covers:
formal service school courses

correspondence courses with proctored end-of-the course examinations

Department of Defense (DOD) courses

Army military occupation specialties

Navy general rates and ratings

APPENDIX

F

Prior Learning Checklist

1. Previous colleges:

Name of College   *Major*   *Approximate Number of Credits*

_____

_____

_____

2. Military service:

Service: _____ Year of discharge: _____

Training (see DD214 form): _____

_____

_____

3. Have you even taken any of the following tests?

CLEP _____ Other

GREs _____

DANTES _____ _____

4. Licenses held: Year received:

_____ _____

_____ _____

_____ _____

5. Apprentice training: Year completed:

_____ _____

_____ _____

_____ _____

6. Other training and nonaccredited courses:

Institution	Year(s)	Topic	Description
_____	_____	_____	_____
_____	_____	_____	_____
_____	_____	_____	_____

Use additional paper if necessary.

7. Job history:

Current Job Title	Years Held	Responsibilities
_____	_____	_____

Former Jobs   *Years Held*   *Responsibilities*

_____   _____   _____

Former Jobs   *Years Held*   *Responsibilities*

_____   _____   _____

Former Jobs   *Years Held*   *Responsibilities*

_____   _____   _____

Use additional paper if necessary.

8. Hobbies: _____

_____

_____

9. Foreign languages:

_____

10. Union involvement and experience:

_____

_____

_____

11. Organizational memberships:

Organization   *Offices Held*

_____   _____

_____   _____

_____   _____

12. Other areas of knowledge gained from reading, study, community involvement, etc.:

_____

_____

_____

_____

G

Learning Assessment
Worksheet

Experience	Time Spent in Activity	Description of Duties, Tasks, and Activities	Description of Learning Outcomes and Competencies	Documentation: Can You Suggest Ways an Evaluator Can Judge These?
Employment				
Education (noncredit courses and seminars)				
Volunteer Experience				
Recreation and Hobbies				

Experience	Time Spent in Activity	Description of Duties, Tasks, and Activities	Description of Learning Outcomes and Competencies	Documentation: Can You Suggest Ways an Evaluator Can Judge These?
Military Experience				
Licenses, Awards, Publications				
Travel				
Professional Readings				

Experience	Time Spent in Activity	Description of Duties, Tasks, and Activities	Description of Learning Outcomes and Competencies	Documentation: Can You Suggest Ways an Evaluator Can Judge These?
Other				
Other				
Other				
Other				

A P P E N D I X

H

Documentation Worksheet

Learning Component	Type of Documentation	Date Sent For	Date Rec'd.	Present Location
Electronics	Navy Discharge Papers			Top drawer of desk
	Letter from boss at B&B Elec.	3/24	4/2	Under DOC in file
Management	Certificate of Course at IBM			Under DOC in file
	Letter from IBM supervisor	3/24	4/16	Top drawer of desk
	Transcript of Atwater College Course in Mgt.	3/27		
	Letter from ACME supervisor	3/24		
Accounting	CLEP Test Transcript	3/11	3/29	Under DOC in file
Painting	Small paintings			Living rm
	Slides			Studio
	Letter from painting teacher	2/26	3/30	Under DOC in file
	Eval. of work by gallery owner	3/27		
Journalism	Eval. of work by Prof. James		4/17	Under DOC in file
	Copies of my news stories, reviews			Basement closet

I

Study Tips

1. Make a schedule of your study time and then stick to it.

2. Plan ahead to accommodate extra study time in weeks when a paper is due or there is an examination.

3. Have prior agreements with your family and friends that your study time is not to be interrupted except for emergencies.

4. Try to study in one particular place that is quiet and well lit (diffused lighting is best).

5. Keep the top of your desk clear of distracting clutter (pictures, magazines, bills, etc.).

6. Take short rests during long study sessions.

7. When you study, work to your maximum ability. Don't dawdle or fool around; give it your all.

8. Start studying as soon as you sit down at your desk.

9. Always make a preliminary survey of your assignment before reading in detail.

10. As you study, evaluate what you are trying to learn. Ask yourself:

    What is it for?

    How does it work?

    Why is it expressed this way?

    When does it happen?

11. Remember that the type in which headings are printed is a clue to the importance of the material.

12. Study all graphs, drawings, and tables; they are placed in the text for a purpose.

13. Be sure you know the meanings of all technical words in the text. If you don't, look them up.

14. Always find the main thought in each paragraph.

15. Try to associate the ideas of the paragraphs and chapters of your assignment.

16. After studying the lesson carefully, summarize the contents in your own words.

17. Use an abbreviated outline form when taking notes.

18. If you own the book, it may be helpful to underline or highlight important ideas, facts, or statements to help you later when you are studying for exams.

19. Footnotes and bibliographies in your textbook may be useful in locating resources for your research papers.

20. Keep all notes on one subject together.

21. Devote one hour a week to a weekly review in each subject.

22. If certain subject matter must be memorized, do not try to do it all at one time.

23. It is generally better to learn from, or memorize, the whole before the details.

24. Apply everything you learn as early and as often as possible.

25. During examination week, maintain regular habits and get your usual amount of sleep. "All nighters" leave you in poor condition to do your best on tests.

26. When taking a test, be sure to read all questions before answering any; outline the answers to essay questions before attempting to write them out.

27. In lectures, do not try to write down the exact words of the instructor, but summarize them in a shorthand you will understand.

28. When in class, pay attention to what is going on or you will miss important parts of the instructor's explanation of the lesson. If your mind starts to wander or you get sleepy, take a few deep breaths, sit up straighter, and LISTEN.

29. Do not skip a class without a compelling reason just because you feel that you can make up the work. However, just in case you cannot attend, keep at hand the phone number of a classmate who can fill you in on what happened, lend you notes, or remind you of due dates for papers and tests. The buddy system is very helpful in an emergency.

30. Do not hesitate to ask your instructor for help if you need it.

APPENDIX

J

Colleges and Universities with Prior Learning Assessment Programs

"For a Nation of Lifelong Learners," a three-year grant funded by the W.K. Kellogg Foundation in 1994, was guided by a steering committee from the Council for Adult and Experiential Learning (CAEL); Regents College, University of the State of New York; Empire State College, New York; and the American Council on Education (ACE). As part of this project, two data bases were developed: the first reflecting current programs serving adult learners and the second, sponsored by CAEL, reflecting current practices in the assessment of prior learning. Data for the second was gathered by survey in 1996.

The institutions listed in this appendix responded to the prior learning assessment survey and indicated that they do provide opportunities for the assessment of prior learning for the award of college credit. Questions on policies or procedures should be directed to the respective college or university.

ALABAMA

Auburn University
Auburn (334) 826-4000

Auburn University at Montgomery
Montgomery (334) 244-3618

Birmingham Southern College
Birmingham (205) 226-4600

Faulkner University
Montgomery (334) 272-5820

Jefferson Davis Community College
Brewton (334) 867-4832

Jefferson State Community College
Birmingham (205) 853-1200

John C. Calhoun State Community
College
Decatur (205) 306-2500

Lurleen B. Wallace State Junior
College
Andalusia (334) 222-6591

Oakwood College
Huntsville (205) 726-7000

Southern Christian University
Montgomery (334) 277-2277

Spring Hill College
Mobile (334) 380-3065

Troy State University at Dothan
Dothan (334) 670-3000

Troy State University at Montgomery
Montgomery (334) 241-9546

Tuskegee University
Tuskegee (334) 727-8011

University of Alabama
Tuscaloosa (205) 348-6000

University of Mobile
Mobile (334) 675-5990

University of Montevallo
Montevallo (205) 665-6001

University of North Alabama
Florence (205) 760-4316

University of South Alabama
Mobile (334) 460-6251

University of West Alabama
Livingston (205) 652-3400

ALASKA

Alaska Pacific University
Anchorage (907) 564-8233

Sheldon Jackson College
Sitka (907) 747-5221

University of Alaska
Fairbanks (907) 474-6396

University of Alaska Anchorage
Anchorage (907) 786-1480

ARIZONA

American Graduate School of
International Management
Glendale (602) 978-7980

Central Arizona College
Coolidge (520) 426-4260

Glendale Community College
Glendale (602) 435-3305

Maricopa County Community
College
Tempe (602) 731-8000

Mesa Community College
Mesa (602) 461-7000

Mohave Community College
Kingman (520) 757-4331

Northern Arizona University
Flagstaff (520) 523-2108

Ottawa University
Tucson (602) 371-1188

Prescott College
Prescott (520) 778-2090

Rio Salado Community College
Tempe (602) 517-8000

University of Phoenix—
Assessment Center
Phoenix (602) 966-9577

University of Phoenix
Phoenix (602) 266-4111

University of Phoenix
Tucson (520) 881-6512

Yavapai College
Prescott (520) 445-7300

ARKANSAS

Arkansas State University
State University   (870) 972-2031

Arkansas Tech University
Russellville   (501) 968-0272

Garland County Community College
Hot Springs   (501) 767-9371

Harding University (Main Campus)
Searcy   (501) 279-4404

Hendrix College
Conway   (501) 329-6811

John Brown University
Siloam Springs   (501) 524-9500

Mississippi County Community
College
Blytheville   (870) 762-1020

NorthWest Arkansas Community
College
Bentonville   (501) 636-9222

Ozarka Technical College
Melbourne   (870) 368-7371

Petit Jean Technical College
Morrilton   (501) 354-2465

Southern Arkansas University
Magnolia   (870) 235-4000

Southern Arkansas University
Technical College
Camden   (870) 574-4500

University of Central Arkansas
Conway   (501) 450-5000

Williams Baptist College
Walnut Ridge   (870) 886-6741

CALIFORNIA

Allan Hancock College
Santa Maria   (805) 922-6966

Art Institute of Southern California
Laguna Beach   (714) 497-3309

Azusa Pacific University
Azusa   (818) 969-3434

Bethany College
Scotts Valley   (408) 438-3800

Biola University
La Mirada   (310) 903-6000

California Institute of Integral Studies
San Francisco   (415) 674-5500

California Institute of the Arts
Valencia   (805) 255-1050

California Lutheran University
Thousand Oaks   (805) 493-3106

California State University—
Monterey Bay
Seaside   (408) 582-3592

Chapman University
Orange   (714) 997-6815

Christian Heritage College
El Cajon   (619) 441-2200

College of Notre Dame
Belmont   (415) 593-1601

The Fielding Institute
Santa Barbara   (805) 687-1099

Holy Names College
Oakland   (510) 436-1000

Humboldt State University
Arcata   (707) 826-6196

La Sierra University
Riverside   (909) 785-2000

Los Angeles Southwest College
Los Angeles   (213) 241-5273

The Master's College
Santa Clarita   (800) 568-6248

Mendocino College
Ukiah   (707) 468-3102

Menlo College
Atherton   (415) 688-3750

National University
La Jolla   (619) 563-7100

New College of California
San Francisco   (415) 241-1300

Pepperdine University
Malibu   (310) 456-4000

Pitzer College
Claremont   (909) 621-8000

St. John's Seminary
Camarillo   (805) 482-2755

St. Mary's College of California
Moraga   (510) 631-4000

San Jose City College
San Jose   (408) 298-2181

Santa Clara University
Santa Clara   (408) 554-4764

San Mateo Community College
District
San Mateo   (415) 574-6550

Scripps College
Claremont   (909) 621-8273

Simpson College
Redding   (916) 224-5600

Southern California Institute of
Architecture
Los Angeles   (310) 574-1123

Stanford University
Stanford   (415) 723-1550

University of Judaism
Bel Air   (310) 476-9777

University of LaVerne
La Verne   (909) 593-3511

University of the Pacific
Stockton   (209) 946-2424

University of Phoenix
Westminster   (714) 261-4437

University of Redlands
Redlands   (909) 793-2121

University of San Francisco
San Francisco   (415) 422-6534

University of Southern California
Los Angeles   (213) 740-4623

University of West Los Angeles
Inglewood   (310) 342-5200

West Hills Community College
Coalinga   (209) 935-0801

Westmont College
Santa Barbara   (805) 565-6000

Woodbury University
Burbank   (818) 767-0888

Yuba College
Marysville   (916) 741-6700

COLORADO

Aims Community College
Greeley   (970) 330-8008

Arapahoe Community College
Littleton   (303) 794-1550

Colorado Christian University
Lakewood   (303) 202-0100

Colorado College
Colorado Springs   (719) 389-6610

Colorado Mountain College
Glenwood Springs   (970) 945-8691

Colorado School of Mines
Golden   (303) 273-3200

Community College of Aurora
Aurora   (303) 360-4700

Community College of Denver
Denver   (303) 556-2600

Front Range Community College
Westminster   (303) 466-8811

Metropolitan State College
Denver   (303) 556-3923

Morgan Community College
Fort Morgan   (970) 867-3081

Nazarene Bible College
Colorado Springs   (719) 596-5110

Pikes Peak Community College
Colorado Springs   (719) 540-7228

Pueblo Community College
Pueblo   (719) 549-3200

Red Rocks Community College
Lakewood   (303) 988-6160

Regis University—Colorado Springs
Colorado Springs   (719) 264-7000

Regis University
Denver   (303) 458-4100

Trinidad State Junior College
Trinidad   (719) 846-5621

University of Denver
Denver   (303) 871-3992

University of Northern Colorado
Greeley   (970) 351-1890

University of Phoenix—Englewood
Englewood   (303) 721-1297

Western State College
Gunnison   (970) 943-0120

CONNECTICUT

Albertus Magnus College
New Haven   (203) 773-8550

Charter Oak State College
Newington   (860) 666-4595

Connecticut College
New London   (860) 439-2068

Hartford Seminary
Hartford   (860) 232-4451

Manchester Community-Technical
  College
Manchester   (860) 647-6000

Naugatuck Valley Community-
  Technical College
Waterbury   (203) 575-8013

Quinebaug Valley Community-
  Technical College
Danielson   (860) 774-1130

Quinnipiac College
Hamden   (203) 288-5251

Sacred Heart University
Fairfield   (203) 371-7999

Three Rivers Community-Technical
  College
Norwich   (860) 886-1931

Trinity College
Hartford   (860) 297-2437

University of Bridgeport
Bridgeport   (203) 576-4000

Western Connecticut State University
Danbury   (203) 837-8200

DELAWARE

Delaware Technical and Community
  College (Central Office)
Dover   (302) 739-3737

Wesley College
Dover   (302) 736-2351

DISTRICT OF COLUMBIA

The American University
Washington, DC   (202) 885-1800

The Catholic University of America
Washington   (202) 319-5000

Gallaudet University
Washington   (202) 651-5393

George Washington University
Washington, DC   (202) 994-6161

Mount Vernon College
Washington   (202) 625-4527

Trinity College
Washington, DC   (202) 884-9000

FLORIDA

Barry University/School of Adult and
  Continuing Education
Miami Shores   (305) 899-3319

Bethune Cookman College
Daytona Beach   (904) 255-1401

Brevard Community College
Cocoa   (407) 632-1111

Broward Community College
Fort Lauderdale   (954) 761-7401

Caribbean Center for Advanced
  Studies/Miami Institute of
  Psychology
Miami   (305) 593-1223

Clearwater Christian College
Clearwater   (813) 726-1153

Eckerd College
St. Petersburg   (813) 864-8226

Embry-Riddle Aeronautical
  University
Daytona Beach   (904) 226-6000

Florida Atlantic University
Boca Raton   (561) 367-3000

Florida Baptist Theological College
Graceville   (904) 263-3261

Florida Community College
Jacksonville   (904) 381-3629

Florida Institute of Technology
Melbourne   (407) 768-8000

Florida International University
Miami   (305) 348-2000

Florida Keys Community College
Key West   (305) 296-9081

Florida Southern College
Lakeland   (941) 680-4111

Florida State University
Tallahassee   (904) 644-5887

International College
Naples   (941) 774-4700
Fort Myers   (941) 482-0019

Lynn University
Boca Raton   (561) 994-0770

Nova Southeastern University
Fort Lauderdale   (954) 475-7300

Palm Beach Atlantic College
West Palm Beach   (561) 803-2000

Pensacola Junior College
Pensacola   (904) 484-1600

Southern College
Orlando   (407) 273-1000

Stetson University
De Land   (904) 822-7000

University of Florida
Gainesville   (352) 392-1374

University of Tampa
Tampa   (813) 253-3333

Warner Southern College
Lake Wales   (941) 638-1462

Webber College
Babson Park   (941) 638-1431

GEORGIA

Abraham Baldwin Agricultural
  College
Tifton   (912) 386-3236

Agnes Scott College
Decatur   (404) 638-6306

Albany State University
Albany   (912) 430-4638

Andrew College
Cuthbert   (912) 732-2171

Armstrong Atlantic State College
Savannah   (912) 927-5277

Augusta Technical Institute
Augusta   (706) 771-4035

Brenau University
Gainesville   (770) 534-6198

Brewton-Parker College
Mount Vernon   (912) 583-2241

Clark Atlanta University
Atlanta   (404) 880-8000

Clayton State College
Morrow   (770) 961-3485

Coastal Georgia Community College
Brunswick   (912) 264-7235

Covenant College
Lookout Mountain   (706) 820-1560

Emmanuel College
Franklin Springs   (706) 245-7226

Georgia State University
Atlanta   (404) 651-2000

Medical College of Georgia
Augusta   (706) 721-2201

North Georgia College
Dahlonega   (706) 864-1750

Oglethorpe University
Atlanta   (404) 261-1441

Piedmont College
Demorest   (706) 778-3000

Reinhardt College
Waleska   (770) 720-5550

Spelman College
Atlanta   (404) 681-3643

Toccoa Falls College
Toccoa Falls   (706) 886-6831

Truett McConnell College
Cleveland   (706) 865-2134

University of Georgia
Athens   (706) 542-6400

Wesleyan College
Macon   (912) 477-1110

HAWAII

Chaminade University of Honolulu
Honolulu   (808) 735-4773

Hawaii Pacific University
Honolulu   (808) 544-9300

University of Hawaii Leeward
  Community College
Pearl City   (808) 455-0423

IDAHO

Boise State University
Boise   (208) 385-1491

Lewis-Clark State College
Lewiston   (208) 799-2210

Northwest Nazarene College
Nampa   (208) 467-8011

Ricks College
Rexburg   (208) 356-1007

ILLINOIS

Augustana College
Rock Island   (309) 794-7277

Aurora University
Aurora   (630) 844-6517

Barat College
Lake Forest (847) 234-3000

Belleville Area College
Belleville (618) 235-2700

Benedictine University
Lisle (630) 960-1500

Carl Sandburg College
Galesburg (309) 344-2518

City Colleges of Chicago
Chicago (312) 553-2500

College of DuPage
Glen Ellyn (630) 942-2316

College of St. Francis
Joliet (815) 740-3360

Columbia College
Chicago (312) 663-1600

Concordia University
River Forest (708) 771-8300

DePaul University
Chicago (312) 362-8001

DeVry Institute of Technology
Addison (630) 953-1300

Elmhurst College
Elmhurst (630) 617-3500

Governors State University
University Park (708) 534-4092

Greenville College
Greenville (618) 664-1840

Illinois College
Jacksonville (217) 245-3000

Illinois Eastern Community College
All campuses (618) 393-2982

Illinois State University
Normal (309) 438-2264

Illinois Wesleyan University
Bloomington (309) 556-3161

John Wood Community College
Quincy (217) 224-6500

Joliet Junior College
Joliet (815) 729-5020

Kankakee Community College
Kankakee (815) 933-0345

Kishwaukee College
Malta (815) 825-2086

Lake Forest College
Lake Forest (847) 735-5026

Lewis University
Romeoville (815) 838-0500

MacMurray College
Jacksonville (217) 479-7000

McKendree College
Lebanon (618) 537-4481

Mennonite College of Nursing
Bloomington (309) 829-0715

Monmouth College
Monmouth (309) 457-2326

Moraine Valley Community College
Palos Hills (708) 974-5710

National—Louis University
Evanston (847) 475-1100

National—Louis University
Wheaton (630) 668-3838

North Central College
Naperville (630) 637-5100

North Park College
Chicago (773) 244-6200

Northwestern University
Evanston (847) 491-5234

Olivet Nazarene University
Kankakee (815) 939-5201

Parks College of St. Louis University
Cahokia (618) 337-7575

Quincy University
Quincy (217) 222-8020

Robert Morris College
Chicago (312) 836-4888

Rockford College
Rockford (815) 226-4070

Roosevelt University
Chicago (312) 341-3521

Rosary College
River Forest (708) 366-2490

St. Xavier University
Chicago (773) 298-3020

St. Joseph College of Nursing
Joliet (815) 741-7123

Trinity Christian College
Palos Heights (708) 597-3000

Trinity International University
Deerfield (847) 317-6500

University of Illinois at Springfield
Springfield (217) 786-6600

Western Illinios University
Macomb   (309) 298-1929

Wheaton College
Wheaton   (630) 752-5044

INDIANA

Bethel College
Mishawaka   (219) 259-8511

Butler University
Indianapolis   (317) 940-9203

Calumet College of St. Joseph
Whiting   (219) 473-7770

De Pauw University
Greencastle   (317) 658-4800

Earlham College
Richmond   (317) 983-1200

Franklin College of Indiana
Franklin   (317) 738-8018

Goshen College
Goshen   (219) 535-7000

Grace College
Winona Lake   (219) 372-5100

Holy Cross College
Notre Dame   (219) 239-8400

Huntington College
Huntington   (219) 356-6000

Indiana Institute of Technology
Fort Wayne   (219) 422-5561

Indiana University
Bloomington   (812) 855-3693

Indiana University
South Bend   (219) 237-4298

Indiana University East
Richmond   (317) 973-8200

Indiana University/Purdue
  University
Indianapolis   (317) 274-4591

Ivy Tech State College—East Central
Muncie   (317) 289-2291

Ivy Tech State College—Lafayette
Lafayette   (317) 772-9100

Ivy Tech State College—Southwest
Evansville   (812) 429-1435

Ivy Tech State College—Whitewater
Richmond   (317) 966-2656

Manchester College
North Manchester   (219) 982-5000

Martin University
Indianapolis   (317) 543-3235

Oakland City University
Oakland City   (812) 749-1412

St. Francis College
Fort Wayne   (219) 434-3100

St. Joseph's College
Rensselaer   (219) 866-6000

St. Mary's College
Notre Dame   (219) 284-4577

St. Mary-of-the-Woods College
St. Mary-of-the-Woods (812) 535-5269

St. Meinrad College
St. Meinrad   (812) 357-6611

Tri-State University
Angola   (219) 665-4210

University of Evansville
Evansville   (812) 479-2981

University of Southern Indiana
Evansville   (812) 464-8600

Vincennes University
Vincennes   (812) 888-5832

Wabash College
Crawfordsville   (317) 361-6244

IOWA

American Institute of Commerce
Davenport   (319) 355-3500

Buena Vista University
Storm Lake   (712) 749-2400

Central College
Pella   (515) 628-5331

Clarke College
Dubuque   (319) 588-6300

Coe College
Cedar Rapids   (319) 399-8526

Cornell College
Mount Vernon   (319) 895-4372

Des Moines Area Community College
Ankeny   (515) 964-6200

Divine Word College
Epworth   (319) 876-3353

Dordt College
Sioux Center   (712) 722-3771

Graceland College
Lamoni   (515) 784-5000

Grinnell College
Grinnell   (515) 269-4000

Indian Hills Community College
Ottumwa   (515) 683-5159

Iowa Lakes Community College
Estherville   (712) 362-2604

Iowa State University
Ames   (515) 294-5836

Iowa Western Community College
Council Bluffs   (712) 325-3400

Loras College
Dubuque   (319) 588-7100

Marycrest International University
Davenport   (319) 326-9512

Morningside College
Sioux City   (712) 274-5100

Mount Mercy College
Cedar Rapids   (319) 363-8213

Mount St. Clare College
Clinton   (319) 242-4023

Northwestern College
Orange City   (712) 737-7000

St. Ambrose University
Davenport   (319) 333-6344

Simpson College
Indianola   (515) 961-6251

Southeastern Community College
West Burlington   (319) 752-2731

University of Dubuque
Dubuque   (312) 589-3200

University of Iowa
Iowa City   (319) 335-0217

Wartburg College
Waverly   (319) 352-8272

Westmar University
Le Mars   (712) 546-7081

KANSAS

Baker University
Overland Park   (913) 491-4432

Barclay College
Haviland   (316) 862-5252

Barton County Community College
Great Bend   (316) 792-2701

Benedictine College
Atchison   (913) 367-5340

Bethel College
North Newton   (316) 283-2500

Butler County Community College
El Dorado   (316) 321-2222

Colby Community College
Colby   (913) 462-3984

Donnelly College
Kansas City   (913) 621-6070

Emporia State University
Emporia   (316) 343-1200

Fort Hays State University
Hays   (913) 628-4000

Hesston College
Hesston   (316) 327-8204

Independence Community College
Independence   (316) 331-4100

Kansas Newman College
Wichita   (316) 942-4291

Kansas State University
Manhattan   (913) 532-6011

Manhattan Christian College
Manhattan   (913) 539-3571

MidAmerica Nazarene College
Olathe   (913) 782-3750

Neosho County Community College
Chanute   (316) 431-2820

Ottawa University—Kansas City
Overland Park   (913) 451-1431

Pittsburg State University
Pittsburg   (316) 231-7000

St. Mary College
Leavenworth   (913) 682-5151

Southwestern College
Winfield   (316) 221-8205

Tabor College
Hillsboro   (316) 947-3121

Tabor College—Wichita
Wichita   (316) 681-8616

University of Kansas
Lawrence   (913) 864-3911

Washburn University of Topeka
Topeka   (913) 231-1010

Wichita State University
Wichita   (316) 978-3085

KENTUCKY

Bellarmine College
Louisville   (502) 452-8133

Brescia College
Owensboro   (502) 686-4241

Cumberland College
Williamsburg   (606) 549-2200

Georgetown College
Georgetown   (502) 863-8024

Hopkinsville Community College
Hopkinsville   (502) 886-3921

Lindsey Wilson College
Columbia   (502) 384-2126

Madisonville Community College
Madisonville   (502) 821-2250

Maysville Community College
Maysville   (606) 759-7141

Midway College
Midway   (606) 846-5778

Murray State University
Murray   (502) 762-3741

Northern Kentucky University
Highland Heights   (606) 572-5100

Owensboro Community College
Owensboro   (502) 686-4400

Prestonsburg Community College
Prestonsburg   (606) 886-3863

Southern Baptist Theological
  Seminary
Louisville   (502) 897-4209

Spalding University
Louisville   (502) 585-9911

Thomas More College
Crestview Hills   (606) 341-5800

Union College
Barbourville   (606) 546-1208

University of Kentucky
Lexington   (606) 257-9000

Western Kentucky University
Bowling Green   (502) 745-3351

LOUISIANA

Delgado Community College
New Orleans   (504) 483-4238

Louisiana College
Pineville   (318) 487-7011

Louisiana State University
Baton Rouge   (504) 388-2070

Louisiana State University at
  Alexandria
Alexandria   (318) 445-3672

Louisiana State University at Eunice
Eunice   (318) 457-7311

McNeese State University
Lake Charles   (318) 475-5000

Nunez Community College
Chalmette   (504) 278-7350

Our Lady of Holy Cross College
New Orleans   (504) 394-7744

University of New Orleans
New Orleans   (504) 280-7393

Xavier University
New Orleans   (504) 483-7425

MAINE

Central Maine Medical Center School
  of Nursing
Lewiston   (207) 795-2840

Maine Maritime Academy
Castnie   (207) 326-2311

Northern Maine Technical College
Presque Isle   (207) 768-2700

St. Joseph's College
Standish   (207) 892-6766

Thomas College
Waterville   (207) 873-0771

University of Maine
Orono   (207) 581-1309

University of Maine at Farmington
Farmington   (207) 778-7050

University of Maine at Fort Kent
Fort Kent   (207) 834-7500

University of Maine System
Bangor   (207) 973-3231

University of New England
Biddeford   (207) 283-0171

University of Southern Maine
Portland   (207) 780-4141

MARYLAND

Anne Arundel Community College
Arnold   (410) 541-2243

Capitol College
Laurel   (301) 369-2800

Cecil Community College
North East   (410) 287-6060

College of Notre Dame of Maryland
Baltimore   (410) 532-5320

Columbia Union College
Takoma Park   (301) 891-4000

Dundalk Community College
Baltimore   (410) 285-9802

Garrett Community College
McHenry   (301) 387-3000

Hood College
Frederick   (301) 663-3131

Howard Community College
Columbia   (410) 992-4800

Johns Hopkins University
Baltimore   (410) 516-8000

Montgomery College—Rockville
  Campus
Rockville   (301) 279-5000

Morgan State University
Baltimore   (410) 319-3000

Mount St. Mary's College and
  Seminary
Emmitsburg   (301) 447-6122

Peabody Institute of Johns Hopkins
  University
Baltimore   (410) 659-8266

Prince George's Community College
Largo   (301) 322-0437

St. Mary's College of Maryland
St. Mary's City   (301) 862-0336

Towson State University
Baltimore   (410) 830-2000

University of Maryland College Park
College Park   (301) 405-1000

University of Maryland University
  College
College Park   (301) 985-7265

Washington College
Chestertown   (410) 778-7299

Western Maryland College
Westminster   (410) 857-2215

MASSACHUSETTS

Assumption College
Worcester   (508) 767-7355

Atlantic Union College
South Lancaster   (508) 368-2304

Bay Path College
Longmeadow   (413) 567-0621

Bentley College
Waltham   (617) 891-2803

Berkshire Community College
Pittsfield   (413) 499-4660

Boston Architectural College
Boston   (617) 536-3170

Boston College
Chestnut Hill   (617) 552-8000

Boston Conservatory
Boston   (617) 536-6340

Bradford College
Bradford   (508) 372-7161

Bridgewater State College
Bridgewater   (508) 697-1200

Bristol Community College
Fall River   (508) 678-2811

Bunker Hill Community College
Boston   (617) 228-2000

Cambridge College
Cambridge   (617) 868-1000

College of Our Lady of the Elms
Chicopee   (413) 594-2761

Emerson College
Boston   (617) 578-8500

Emmanuel College
Boston   (617) 227-9340

Fitchburg State College
Fitchburg   (508) 665-3137

Hellenic College-Holy Cross Greek
  Orthodox School of Theology
Brookline   (617) 731-3500

Holyoke Community College
Holyoke   (413) 538-7000

Lesley College
Cambridge   (617) 868-9600

Marian Court College
Swampscott   (617) 595-6768

Massachusetts Maritime Academy
Buzzards Bay   (508) 830-5000

Massasoit Community College
Brockton   (508) 588-9100

Mount Holyoke College
South Hadley   (413) 538-2025

Nichols College
Dudley   (508) 943-1560

North Shore Community College
Danvers   (508) 762-4000

Northeastern University—University
  College
Boston   (617) 373-2400

Pine Manor College
Chestnut Hill   (617) 731-7135

Quinsigamond Community College
Worcester   (508) 853-2300

Salem State College
Salem   (508) 741-6000

Smith College
Northampton   (413) 585-2550

Springfield College
Springfield   (413) 748-3579

Springfield Technical Community
  College
Springfield   (413) 781-7822

Stonehill College
North Easton   (508) 565-1000

University of Massachusetts
Amherst   (413) 545-0222

Wentworth Institute of Technology
Boston   (617) 442-9010

MICHIGAN

Albion College
Albion   (517) 629-0477

Baker College of Port Huron
Port Huron   (810) 985-7000

Calvin College
Grand Rapids   (616) 957-6000

Center for Creative Studies—College
  of Art and Design
Detroit   (313) 872-3118

Central Michigan University
Mt. Pleasant   (517) 774-3865

Concordia College
Ann Arbor   (313) 995-7300

Cornerstone College and Grand
  Rapids Baptist Seminary
Grand Rapids   (616) 949-5300

Davenport College
Grand Rapids   (616) 732-1070

Detroit College of Business
Dearborn   (313) 581-4400

Eastern Michigan University
Ypsilanti   (313) 487-2128

Ferris State University
Big Rapids   (616) 592-2000

G M I Engineering & Management
  Institute
Flint   (810) 762-9500

Glen Oaks Community College
Centreville   (616) 467-9945

Grand Rapids Community College
Grand Rapids   (616) 771-4000

Grand Valley State University
Allendale   (616) 895-2025

Great Lakes Junior College
Saginaw   (517) 755-3457

Hillsdale College
Hillsdale   (517) 437-7341

Kellogg Community College
Battle Creek   (616) 965-3931

Kirtland Community College
Roscommon   (517) 275-5121

Lake Michigan College
Benton Harbor   (616) 927-8100

Lake Superior State University
Sault Sainte Marie   (906) 635-2680

Lansing Community College
Lansing   (517) 483-1200

Lawrence Technological University
Southfield   (810) 204-4000

Madonna University
Livonia   (313) 591-5000

Michigan Christian College
Rochester Hills   (810) 651-5800

Michigan State University
East Lansing   (517) 355-1855

Montcalm Community College
Sidney   (517) 328-2111

Northwestern Michigan College
Traverse City   (616) 922-1000

Northwood University
Midland   (517) 837-4455

Oakland Community College
Bloomfield Hills   (810) 540-1500

Reformed Bible College
Grand Rapids   (616) 222-3000

Saginaw Valley State University
University Center   (517) 790-4000

St. Mary's College
Orchard Lake   (810) 682-1885

Schoolcraft College
Livonia   (313) 462-4400

Spring Arbor College
Spring Arbor   (517) 750-1200

Suomi College
Hancock   (906) 482-5300

Wayne State University
Detroit   (313) 577-2424

MINNESOTA

Bethany Lutheran College
Mankato   (507) 386-5130

Cardinal Stritch College
Minneapolis   (612) 835-6418

Century College
White Bear Lake   (612) 779-3200

College of St. Benedict
St. Joseph   (320) 363-3395

College of St. Catherine
St. Paul   (612) 690-6000

Concordia College—Moorhead
Moorhead   (218) 299-3250

Concordia College—St. Paul
St. Paul   (612) 641-8233

Dakota County Technical College
Rosemount   (612) 423-8216

Gustavus Adolphus College
St. Peter   (507) 933-7495

Macalester College
St. Paul   (612) 696-6000

Mankato State University
Mankato   (507) 389-2463

Martin Luther College
New Ulm   (507) 354-8221

Metropolitan State University
Saint Paul   (612) 772-7721

Minneapolis Community and
  Technical College
Minneapolis   (612) 341-7040

Minnesota Bible College
Rochester   (507) 288-4563

Moorhead State University
Moorhead   (218) 236-2011

Normandale Community College
Bloomington   (612) 832-6314

North Central Bible College
Minneapolis   (612) 343-4409

Northland Community and Technical
  College
Thief River Falls   (218) 681-0701

Northwest Technical Colleges
All Campuses   (218) 773-4506

Riverland Community College
Albert Lea   (507) 373-0656

St. Cloud Technical College
St. Cloud   (320) 654-5075

Saint Mary's University of Minnesota
Winona   (612) 874-9877

St. John's University
Collegeville   (320) 252-0101

University of Minnesota—Duluth
Duluth   (218) 726-7849

University of Minnesota—Twin Cities
  Program for Industrial Leadership
Minneapolis   (612) 624-4020

University of Saint Thomas
Saint Paul   (612) 962-6700

MISSISSIPPI

Belhaven College
Jackson   (601) 968-5916

Blue Mountain College
Blue Mountain   (601) 685-4771

Mississippi College
Clinton   (601) 925-3210

Mississippi Gulf Coast Community
  College
Perkinston   (601) 928-5211

Mississippi State University
Mississippi State   (601) 325-1913

Mississippi University for Women
Columbus   (601) 329-4750

Southwest Mississippi Community
College
Summit   (601) 276-2000

Tougaloo College
Tougaloo   (601) 977-6156

MISSOURI

Berean University
Springfield   (800) 443-1083

Central Methodist College
Fayette   (816) 248-3391

Central Missouri State University
Warrensburg   (816) 543-4900

College of the Ozarks
Point Lookout   (417) 334-6411

Crowder College
Neosho   (417) 451-3223

Culver-Stockton College
Canton   (217) 231-6000

Deaconess College of Nursing
St. Louis   (314) 768-3039

East Central College
Union   (314) 583-5193

Fontbonne College
St. Louis   (314) 862-3456

Hannibal-La Grange College
Hannibal   (573) 221-3675

Harris-Stowe State College
St. Louis   (314) 340-3366

Logan College of Chiropractic
Chesterfield   (314) 227-2100

Midwest College & Seminary
Wentzville   (314) 327-4645

Missouri Southern State College
Joplin   (417) 625-9340

Missouri Valley College
Marshall   (816) 886-6924

North Central Missouri College
Trenton   (816) 359-3948

Park College
Parkville   (816) 741-2000

Phillips Junior College
Springfield   (417) 864-7220

Rockhurst College
Kansas City   (816) 501-4000

St. Louis University
St. Louis   (314) 977-2222

Southeast Missouri State University
Cape Girardeau   (573) 651-2000

Southwest Baptist University
Bolivar   (417) 326-5281

St. Charles County Community
College
St. Peters   (314) 922-8000

Stephens College
Columbia   (573) 442-2211

Three Rivers Community College
Poplar Bluff   (573) 840-9600

University of Missouri—Kansas City
Kansas City   (816) 235-1000

Webster University
St. Louis   (314) 968-6913

Webster University
Webster Groves   (314) 968-6900

William Jewell College
Liberty   (816) 781-7700

William Woods University
Fulton   (573) 592-1149

MONTANA

Carroll College
Helena   (406) 447-4300

Dawson Community College
Glendive   (406) 365-3396

Montana State University—Billings
Billings   (406) 657-2011

Montana State University—Bozeman
Bozeman   (406) 994-2601

Montana State University—Northern
Havre   (406) 265-3701

Montana State University College of
Technology—Great Falls
Great Falls   (406) 771-4300

Montana Tech of The University of
Montana
Butte   (406) 496-4101

Rocky Mountain College
Billings   (406) 657-1030

University of Montana
Missoula   (406) 243-6266

Western Montana College
Dillon   (406) 683-7011

NEBRASKA

Bellevue University
Bellevue   (402) 293-3712

Clarkson College
Omaha   (402) 552-2543

College of St. Mary
Omaha   (402) 399-2400

Creighton University
Omaha   (402) 280-2702

Metropolitan Community College
Omaha   (402) 449-8400

Midland Lutheran College
Fremont   (402) 721-5480

Nebraska Wesleyan
Lincoln   (402) 466-2371

Northeast Community College
Norfolk   (402) 371-2020

University of Nebraska—Lincoln
Lincoln   (402) 472-7211

University of Nebraska at Kearney
Kearney   (308) 865-8209

University of Nebraska Medical
  Center
Omaha   (402) 559-4206

Western Nebraska Community
  College
Scotts Bluff   (308) 635-3606

York College
York   (402) 363-5600

NEVADA

Sierra Nevada College
Incline Village   (702) 831-1314

NEW HAMPSHIRE

Antioch University/New England
Keene   (603) 357-3122

College for Lifelong Learning
Concord   (603) 228-3000

Dartmouth College
Hanover   (603) 646-2246

Franklin Pierce College
Rindge   (603) 899-4094

New England College
Henniker   (603) 428-2203

New Hampshire College
Manchester   (603) 668-2211

New Hampshire Technical College at
  Manchester
Manchester   (603) 668-6706

Notre Dame College
Manchester   (603) 669-4298

Plymouth State College
Plymouth   (603) 535-5000

Rivier College
Nashua   (603) 888-1311

University of New Hampshire
Durham   (603) 862-1234

NEW JERSEY

The College of New Jersey
Trenton   (609) 771-2141

College of St. Elizabeth
Morristown   (201) 605-7441

Georgian Court College
Lakewood   (908) 364-2200

Mercer County Community College
Trenton   (609) 586-4800

Middlesex County College
Edison   (908) 548-6000

Montclair State University
Upper Montclair   (201) 655-4000

Ramapo College of New Jersey
Mahwah   (201) 529-7695

Raritan Valley Community College
Somerville   (908) 526-8358

Richard Stockton College of New
  Jersey
Pomona   (609) 652-1776

Salem Community College
Carneys Point   (609) 299-2100

State University of New Jersey
Rutgers Central Office
New Brunswick   (908) 932-1766

Thomas A. Edison State College
Trenton   (609) 984-1100

Union County College
Cranford   (908) 709-7127

William Paterson College
Wayne   (201) 595-2000

NEW MEXICO

College of Santa Fe
Santa Fe   (505) 473-6011

College of the Southwest
Hobbs   (505) 392-6561

National College
Albuquerque   (505) 265-7517

New Mexico Junior College
Hobbs   (505) 392-5092

New Mexico Military Institute
Roswell   (505) 624-8070

Northern New Mexico Community
College
Espanola   (505) 747-2100

Santa Fe Community College
Santa Fe   (505) 471-8200

University of Phoenix—Albuquerque
Albuquerque   (505) 821-4800

Western New Mexico University
Silver City   (505) 538-6118

NEW YORK

Barnard College
New York City   (212) 854-2011

Brooklyn College
Brooklyn   (718) 951-5911

Broome Community College
Binghamton   (607) 778-5000

Canisius College
Buffalo   (716) 888-2990

City University of New York/College
of Staten Island
Staten Island   (718) 982-2000

City University of New York Herbert
H. Lehman College
Bronx   (718) 960-8105

Clinton Community College
Plattsburgh   (518) 562-4122

Colgate University
Hamilton   (315) 824-7406

College of Mount St. Vincent
Riverdale   (718) 405-3200

College of New Rochelle
New Rochelle   (914) 654-5854

College of St. Rose
Albany   (518) 454-9211

Concordia College
Bronxville   (914) 337-9300

Crouse-Irving Memorial Hospital
School of Nursing
Syracuse   (315) 470-7481

D'Youville College
Buffalo   (716) 881-3200

Daemen College
Amherst   (716) 839-3600

Dominican College of Blauvelt
Orangeburg   (914) 359-7800

Empire State College of the State
University of New York
Saratoga Springs   (518) 587-2100

Erie Community College—South
Campus
Orchard Park   (716) 851-1668

Finger Lakes Community College
Canandaigua   (716) 394-3500

Fordham University
Bronx   (718) 817-3900

Fulton-Montgomery Community
College
Johnstown   (518) 762-4651

Genesee Community College
Batavia   (716) 343-0055

Hamilton College
Clinton   (315) 859-4637

Hartwick College
Oneonta   (607) 431-4200

Hilbert College
Hamburg   (716) 649-7900

Hofstra University
Hempstead   (516) 463-6600

Houghton College
Houghton   (716) 567-9200

Houghton College
West Seneca   (716) 674-6363

Hudson Valley Community College
Troy   (518) 270-1569

Interboro Institute
New York   (212) 399-0091

Iona College
New Rochelle   (914) 633-2000

Ithaca College
Ithaca   (607) 274-3127

Jefferson Community College
Watertown   (315) 786-2200

Keuka College
Keuka Park   (315) 536-4411

LaGuardia Community College
Long Island City   (718) 482-7232

Manhattan College
Riverdale   (718) 862-8000

Marist College
Poughkeepsie   (914) 575-3250

Marymount College
Tarrytown   (914) 631-3200

Marymount Manhattan College
New York   (212) 517-0600

Molloy College
Rockville Centre   (516) 678-5000

Mount St. Mary College
Newburgh   (914) 561-0800

Nassau Community College
Garden City   (516) 572-8160

Nyack College
Nyack   (914) 358-5360

New School for Social Research
New York   (212) 229-5600

New York Institute of Technology
  Main Campus
Old Westbury   (516) 686-7520

New York University School of
  Continuing Education, Adult
  Degree Studies Division
New York   (212) 998-7107

Niagara University
Niagara   (716) 286-8181

Pace University—New York Campus
New York   (212) 346-1200

Paul Smith's College of Arts and
  Sciences
Paul Smiths   (518) 327-6000

Purchase College, State University of
  New York
Purchase   (914) 251-6000

Regents College of the University of
  the State of New York
Albany   (518) 464-8500

Rensselaer Polytechnic Institute
Troy   (518) 276-6000

Roberts Wesleyan College
Rochester   (716) 594-6000

Rochester Business Institute
Rochester   (716) 266-0430

Rochester Institute of Technology
Rochester   (716) 475-2411

St. Bonaventure University
St. Bonaventure   (716) 375-2000

St. Joseph's College
Patchogue   (516) 447-3248

St. Joseph's College, New York
Brooklyn   (718) 399-0068

Sarah Lawrence College
Bronxville   (914) 395-2302

Schenectady County Community
  College
Schenectady   (518) 346-6211

Siena College
Loudonville   (518) 783-2310

St. Francis College
Brooklyn   (718) 522-2300

St. John Fisher College
Rochester   (716) 385-8000

St. Joseph's Hospital Health Center
  School of Nursing
Syracuse   (315) 448-5046

St. Lawrence University
Canton   (315) 379-5011

St. Thomas Aquinas College
Sparkill   (914) 398-4000

State University of New York
  Colleges at Brockport
Brockport   (716) 395-2211

State University of New York College
  at Geneseo
Geneseo   (716) 245-5566

State University of New York College
at Old Westbury
Old Westbury   (516) 876-3000

State University of New York College
at Oneonta
Oneonta   (607) 436-3500

State University of New York College
at Potsdam
Potsdam   (315) 267-2237

State University of New York College
of Agriculture and Technology at
Cobleskill
Cobleskill   (518) 234-5521

State University of New York College
of Environmental Science and
Forestry
Syracuse   (315) 470-6500

State University of New York College
of Technology at Alfred
Alfred   (607) 587-4796

State University of New York Empire
State College
Saratoga Springs   (518) 587-2100

State University of New York Health
Science Center at Syracuse
Syracuse   (315) 464-4570

State University of New York
Institute of Technology at Utica
Utica   (315) 792-7500

Suffok Community College
Selden   (516) 451-4110

Syracuse University
Syracuse   (315) 443-1034

Trocaire College
Buffalo   (716) 826-1200

Ulster County Community College
Stone Ridge   (914) 687-5083

United States Merchant Marine
Academy
Kings Point   (516) 773-5485

Utica College of Syracuse University
Utica   (315) 792-3195

Villa Maria College of Buffalo
Buffalo   (716) 896-0700

Wells College
Aurora   (315) 364-3770

NORTH CAROLINA

Beaufort County Community College
Washington   (919) 946-6194

Cabarrus College of Health Sciences
Concord   (704) 783-1555

Campbell University
Buies Creek   (910) 893-1200

Carteret Community College
Morehead City   (919) 247-6000

Catawba College
Salisbury   (704) 637-4411

Central Carolina Community College
Sanford   (919) 775-5401

Chowan College
Murfreesboro   (919) 398-4101

Coastal Carolina Community College
Jacksonville   (910) 455-1221

College of the Albemarle
Elizabeth City   (919) 335-0821

Craven Community College
New Bern   (919) 638-4131

Elizabeth City State University
Elizabeth City   (919) 335-3300

Fayetteville Technical Community
College
Fayetteville   (910) 678-8325

Gardner-Webb University
Boiling Springs   (704) 434-4260

Gaston College
Dallas   (704) 922-6231

Greensboro College
Greensboro   (910) 272-7102

Guilford College
Greensboro   (910) 316-2000

Guilford Technical Community
College
Jamestown   (910) 334-4822

Haywood Community College
Clyde   (704) 627-2821

High Point University
High Point   (910) 841-9100

James Sprunt Community College
Kenansville   (910) 296-2400

John Wesley College
High Point   (910) 889-2262

Johnson C. Smith University
Charlotte   (704) 378-1000

Lenoir-Rhyne College
Hickory   (708) 328-7402

Louise Harkey School of Nursing
Concord   (704) 783-1555

Mars Hill College
Mars Hill   (704) 689-1111

Methodist College
Fayetteville   (910) 630-7036

Nash Community College
Rocky Mount   (919) 443-4011

North Carolina Central University
Durham   (919) 560-6066

Pembroke State University
Pembroke   (910) 521-6000

Pfeiffer University
Misenheimer   (704) 463-1360

Pitt Community College
Greenville   (919) 321-4200

Richmond Community College
Hamlet   (919) 582-7000

Roanoke-Chowan Community
  College
Ahoskie   (919) 332-5921

Robeson Community College
Lumberton   (910) 738-7101

Salem College
Winston-Salem   (910) 721-2621

Sandhills Community College
Pinehurst   (910) 692-6185

Surry Community College
Dobson   (910) 386-8121

University of North Carolina at
  Asheville
Asheville   (704) 251-6575

University of North Carolina at
  Wilmington
Wilmington   (910) 962-3243

Western Carolina University
Cullowhee   (704) 227-7317

Western Piedmont Community
  College
Morganton   (704) 438-6000

Wilson Technical Community College
Wilson   (919) 291-1195

Wingate University
Wingate   (704) 233-8000

Winston-Salem State University
Winston-Salem   (910) 750-2000

NORTH DAKOTA

Dickinson State University
Dickinson   (701) 227-2331

Jamestown College
Jamestown   (701) 252-3467

Medcenter One College of Nursing
Bismarck   (701) 224-6271

North Dakota State University Main
  Campus
Fargo   (701) 231-7989

Trinity Bible College
Ellendale   (701) 349-3621

University of Mary
Bismarck   (701) 255-7500

University of North Dakota Main
  Campus
Grand Forks   (701) 777-3821

Valley City State University
Valley City   (701) 845-7295

OHIO

Antioch University
Yellow Springs   (800) 543-9436

Ashland University
Ashland   (419) 289-4142

Baldwin-Wallace College
Berea   (216) 826-2126

Baldwin-Wallace College
Cleveland   (216) 826-2121

Bluffton College
Bluffton   (419) 358-3322

Bowling Green State University
Bowling Green   (419) 372-8441

Capital University
Columbus   (614) 236-6374

Central Ohio Technical College
Newark   (614) 366-1351

Clark State Community College
Springfield   (513) 325-0691

Cleveland State University
Cleveland   (216) 687-2100

College of Wooster
Wooster   (216) 263-2000

Columbus State Community College
Columbus   (614) 227-2400

Denison University
Granville   (614) 587-0810

Franciscan University of Steubenville
Steubenville   (614) 283-3771

Franklin University
Columbus   (614) 341-6237

Heidelberg College
Tiffin   (419) 448-2000

Hiram College
Hiram   (330) 569-5163

Hocking Technical College
Nelsonville   (614) 753-3591

John Carroll University
Cleveland   (216) 397-1886

Kent State University—Main Campus
Kent   (216) 672-3131

Kent State University—Stark Campus
Canton   (330) 499-9600

Kent State University—Trumbull
Campus
Warren   (216) 678-4281

Kenyon College
Gambier   (614) 427-5000

Lake Erie College
Painesville   (216) 352-3361

Lorain County Community College
Elyria   (216) 365-5222

Lourdes College
Sylvania   (419) 885-3211

Marietta College
Marietta   (614) 376-4733

Miami University
Oxford   (513) 529-1809

Mount Union College
Alliance   (330) 823-6586

Mount Vernon Nazarene College
Mount Vernon   (614) 397-6862

Muskingum College
New Concord   (614) 826-8165

North Central Technical College
Mansfield   (419) 755-4800

Northwestern College
Lima   (419) 227-3107

Ohio College of Podiatric Medicine
Cleveland   (216) 231-3300

Ohio Dominican College
Columbus   (614) 253-2741

Ohio State University
Columbus   (614) 292-3980

Ohio University—Eastern Campus
St. Clairsville   (614) 695-1720

Ohio University—Main Campus
Athens   (800) 444-2420

Ohio Wesleyan University
Delaware   (614) 368-3200

Owens Community College
Toledo   (419) 661-7777

Shawnee State University
Portsmouth   (614) 355-2207

Sinclair Community College
Dayton   (513) 226-2500

Southern State Community College
Hillsboro   (513) 393-3431

Tiffin University
Tiffin   (419) 448-3445

Union Institute
Cincinnati   (513) 861-6400

The University Of Akron, Main
Campus
Akron   (216) 972-7111

University of Cincinnati
Cincinnati   (513) 556-9196

Ursuline College
Cleveland   (216) 449-4200

Walsh University
Canton   (330) 499-7090

Washington State Community College
Marietta   (614) 374-8716

Wilberforce University
Wilberforce   (513) 376-2911

Wittenberg University
Springfield   (513) 327-6131

Wright State University—Main
Campus
Dayton   (513) 873-3333

Xavier University
Cincinnati   (513) 745-3000

OKLAHOMA

Cameron University
Lawton   (405) 581-2230

Mid-America Bible College
Oklahoma City   (405) 692-3161

Northeastern State University
Tahlequah   (918) 456-5511

Oklahoma Christian University
Oklahoma City   (405) 425-5000

Oklahoma State University Main
Campus
Stillwater   (405) 744-5000

Oral Roberts University
Oklahoma City   (405) 425-5000

Southeastern Oklahoma State
University
Durant   (405) 924-0121

Southern Nazarene University
Bethany   (405) 789-6400

Southwestern Oklahoma State
University
Weatherford   (405) 774-3778

University of Tulsa
Tulsa   (918) 631-2359

Western Oklahoma State College
Altus   (405) 477-2000

OREGON

Chemeketa Community College
Salem   (503) 399-5000

Concordia University
Portland   (503) 280-8510

Eastern Oregon State College
LaGrande   (541) 962-3519

Eugene Bible College
Eugene   (541) 485-1780

George Fox College
Newberg   (503) 538-8383

Lane Community College
Eugene   (503) 726-2213

Linfield College
McMinnville   (503) 434-2507

Marylhurst College for Lifelong
Learning
Marylhurst   (503) 636-8141

Mt. Hood Community College
Gresham   (503) 667-7392

Multnomah Bible College and Bible
Seminary
Portland   (503) 255-0332

Northwest Christian College
Eugene   (503) 343-1641

Oregon Institute of Technology
Klamath Falls   (541) 885-1000

Pacific University
Forest Grove   (503) 359-2234

Portland State University
Portland   (503) 725-3000

Southwestern Oregon Community
College
Coos Bay   (503) 888-7339

Umpqua Community College
Roseburg   (503) 440-4600

Warner Pacific College
Portland   (503) 775-4366

Western Baptist College
Salem   (503) 581-8600

Western Oregon State College
Monmouth   (503) 838-8000

PENNSYLVANIA

Albright College
Reading   (610) 921-2381

Allentown College of St. Francis De
Salles
Center Valley   (610) 282-1100

Alvernia College
Reading   (610) 796-8200

Baptist Bible College and Seminary
Clarks Summit   (717) 586-2400

Beaver College
Glenside   (215) 572-2100

Bloomsburg University of
Pennsylvania
Bloomsburg   (717) 389-4000

Bryn Mawr College
Bryn Mawr   (610) 526-5140

Bucknell University
Lewisburg   (717) 523-1271

Butler Community College
Butler   (412) 287-8711

Cabrini College
Radnor   (610) 902-8545

Carlow College
Pittsburgh   (412) 578-6000

College Misericordia
Dallas   (717) 674-6400

Delaware County Community
    College
Media   (610) 359-5322

Delaware Valley College
Doylestown   (215) 345-1500

Dickinson College
Carlisle   (717) 243-5121

Drexel University
Philadelphia   (215) 895-2000

East Stroudsburg University of
    Pennsylvania
East Stroudsburg   (717) 424-3148

Eastern College
St. Davids   (610) 341-5854

Eastern College
Wynnewood   (610) 645-5565

Edinboro University of Pennsylvania
Edinboro   (814) 732-2717

Elizabethtown College
Elizabethtown   (717) 361-1422

Franklin & Marshall College
Lancaster   (717) 291-4168

Geneva College
Beaver Falls   (412) 847-6603

Gwynedd-Mercy College
Gwynedd Valley   (215) 646-7300

Harrisburg Area Community College
Harrisburg   (717) 780-2378

Holy Family College
Philadelphia   (215) 637-7700

Immaculata College
Immaculata   (610) 647-4400

Keystone College
La Plume   (717) 945-5141

King's College
Wilkes-Barre   (717) 826-5870

La Roche College
Pittsburgh   (412) 367-9300

La Salle University
Philadelphia   (215) 951-1020

Lackawanna Junior College
Scranton   (717) 961-7840

Lancaster Bible College
Lancaster   (717) 569-7071

Lebanon Valley College
Annville   (717) 867-6100

Lycoming College
Williamsport   (717) 321-4000

Marywood College
Scranton   (717) 348-6281

Messiah College
Grantham   (717) 691-6000

Moravian College
Bethlehem   (610) 861-1300

Mount Aloysius College
Cresson   (814) 886-6383

Muhlenberg College
Allentown   (610) 821-3300

Neumann College
Aston   (610) 455-0505

Northampton County Area
    Community College
Bethlehem   (610) 861-5494

Peirce College
Philadelphia   (215) 545-6400

Pennsylvania College of Podiatric
    Medicine
Philadelphia   (800) 220-3338

Pennsylvania Institute of Technology
Media   (610) 565-7900

Pennsylvania State University Main
    Campus
University Park   (814) 865-6357

Philadelphia College of Bible Studies
Langhorne Manor   (215) 702-4294

Point Park College
Pittsburgh   (412) 392-3861

Reading Area Community College
Reading   (215) 372-4721

Robert Morris College
Coraopolis   (412) 262-8256

Rosemont College
Rosemont   (610) 526-2955

St. Joseph's University
Philadelphia   (610) 660-1000

St. Vincent College & Seminary
Latrobe   (412) 539-9761

Slippery Rock University of
Pennsylvania
Slippery Rock   (412) 738-0512

Susquehanna University
Selinsgrove   (717) 374-0101

Swarthmore College
Swarthmore   (610) 328-8000

Temple University
Philadelphia   (215) 204-7000

Thiel College
Greenville   (412) 589-2110

University of Pittsburgh at Bradford
Bradford   (814) 362-7600

University of Scranton
Scranton   (717) 941-4330

Valley Forge Military College
Wayne   (610) 989-1450

Villanova University
Villanova   (610) 519-4032

Washington and Jefferson College
Washington   (412) 223-6052

Waynesburg College
Waynesburg   (412) 627-8191

Widener University
Chester   (610) 499-4334

York College of Pennsylvania
York   (717) 846-7788

PUERTO RICO

Columbia College
Caguas   (787) 743-4041

Inter American University of Puerto
Rico Central Office
San Juan   (787) 766-1912

Universidad Metropolitana
Rio Piedras   (787) 766-1717

University of Puerto Rico—Cayey
University College
Cayey   (787) 738-2160

University of Puerto Rico—Rio
Piedras Campus
Rio Piedras   (787) 765-6385

University of the Sacred Heart
Santurce   (787) 728-1515

RHODE ISLAND

Community College of Rhode Island
Warwick   (401) 825-2147

New England Institute of Technology
Warwick   (401) 739-5000

Roger Williams University
Bristol   (401) 254-3231

Rhode Island College
Providence   (401) 456-8234

University of Rhode Island
Providence   (401) 277-5160

SOUTH CAROLINA

Aiken Technical College
Aiken   (803) 593-9231

Clemson University
Clemson   (864) 656-3413

Coker College
Hartsville   (803) 383-8000

Columbia College
Columbia   (803) 786-3787

Columbia International University
Columbia   (800) 777-2227

Converse College
Spartanburg   (864) 596-9094

Furman University
Greenville   (864) 294-2000

Greenville Technical College
Greenville   (864) 250-8114

Horry-Georgetown Technical College
Conway   (803) 349-5244

Limestone College
Gaffney   (864) 489-7151

Newberry College
Newberry   (803) 321-5124

Spartanburg Methodist College
Spartanburg   (864) 587-4232

Tri-County Technical College
Pendleton   (864) 646-8361

Trident Technical College
Charleston   (803) 572-6111

University of South Carolina—
  Spartanburg
Spartanburg   (864) 599-2000

Wofford College
Spartanburg   (864) 597-4000

SOUTH DAKOTA

Augustana College
Sioux Falls   (605) 336-5417

Black Hills State University
Spearfish   (605) 642-6262

Dakota State University
Madison   (605) 256-5143

Huron University
Huron   (605) 352-8721

Kilian Community College
Sioux Falls   (605) 336-1711

National College
Rapid City   (605) 394-4800

Northern State University
Aberdeen   (605) 626-3011

Presentation College
Aberdeen   (605) 229-8426

South Dakota School of Mines and
  Technology
Rapid City   (605) 394-2416

South Dakota State University
Brookings   (605) 688-4217

University of Sioux Falls
Sioux Falls   (605) 331-5000

University of South Dakota
Sioux Falls   (605) 367-5646

TENNESSEE

Aquinas College
Nashville   (615) 297-7545

Austin Peay State University
Clarksville   (615) 648-7121

Belmont University
Nashville   (615) 460-7001

Bethel College
McKenzie   (901) 352-1000

Carson-Newman College
Jefferson City   (423) 475-9061

Cleveland State Community College
Cleveland   (423) 540-2722

Cumberland University
Lebanon   (615) 444-2562

Dyersburg State Community College
Dyersburg   (901) 286-3200

East Tennessee State University
Johnson City   (423) 439-1000

Freed-Hardeman University
Henderson   (901) 989-6000

King College
Bristol   (423) 986-1187

Lambuth University
Jackson   (901) 425-3207

Lane College
Jackson   (901) 426-7500

Lincoln Memorial University
Harrogate   (615) 869-3611

Maryville College
Maryville   (423) 981-8000

Middle Tennessee State University
Murfreesboro   (615) 898-2300

Milligan College
Milligan   (423) 461-8700

North Central Institute
Clarkville   (615) 552-6200

Southern College of Seventh Day
  Adventist
Collegedale   (423) 238-2111

State Technical Institute at Memphis
Memphis   (901) 383-4190

Tennessee Wesleyan College
Athens   (423) 745-7504

Trevecca Nazarene University
Nashville   (615) 248-1200

Tusculum College
Greenville   (423) 636-7300

University of Tennessee at
  Chattanooga
Chattanooga   (423) 755-4416

University of Tennessee, Knoxville
Knoxville   (423) 974-2184

The University of Tennessee at Martin
Martin   (901) 587-7053

TEXAS

Abilene Christian University
Abilene   (915) 674-2000

Alvin Community College
Alvin   (713) 331-6111

Baylor College of Medicine
Houston   (713) 798-4951

Baylor University
Waco   (817) 755-1011

Blinn College
Brenham   (409) 830-4000

Cedar Valley College
Lancaster   (214) 860-8250

Central Texas College
Killeen   (817) 526-7161

Collin County Community College
McKinney   (972) 548-6742

Dallas Baptist University
Dallas   (214) 333-7100

Eastfield College
Mesquite   (214) 860-7100

El Centro College
Dallas   (214) 860-2311

Hardin-Simmons University
Abilene   (915) 670-1200

Houston Community College
Houston   (713) 718-5000

Howard College
Big Spring   (915) 264-5000

Howard Payne University
Brownwood   (915) 646-2502

Jarvis Christian College
Hawkins   (903) 769-5724

Lamar University—Beaumont
Beaumont   (409) 880-8209

Laredo Community College
Laredo   (210) 721-5129

Letourneau University
Longview   (903) 233-3250

McMurry University
Abilene   (915) 691-6400

Midland College
Midland   (915) 685-4500

Midwestern State University
Wichita Falls   (817) 689-4000

Mountain View College
Dallas   (214) 860-8600

North Harris Montgomery
  Community College District
Houston   (713) 443-5400

Our Lady of the Lake University
San Antonio   (210) 434-6711

Sam Houston State University
Huntsville   (409) 294-1111

Southwestern Adventist College
Keane   (817) 645-3921

Southwestern University
Georgetown   (512) 863-6511

St. Edward's University
Austin   (512) 416-5897

Stephen F. Austin State University
Nacogdoches   (409) 468-2504

Texas A&M University
College Station   (409) 845-1031

Texas A & M University
Texarkana   (903) 223-3030

Texas Christian University
Fort Worth   (817) 921-1000

Texas Lutheran University
Seguin   (210) 372-8000

Texas Tech University
Lubbock   (806) 742-3652

Texas Wesleyan University
Ft. Worth   (817) 531-4444

Trinity University
San Antonio   (210) 736-7201

Trinity Valley Community College
Athens   (903) 675-6217

Tyler Junior College
Tyler   (903) 510-2523

University of Mary Hardin—Baylor
Belton   (817) 939-4510

University of Texas at Austin
Austin   (512) 475-7399

University of Texas at Dallas
Richardson   (214) 883-2341

University of Texas at El Paso
El Paso   (915) 747-5000

Vernon Regional Junior College
Vernon   (817) 552-6291

Victoria College
Victoria   (512) 573-3291

Wayland Baptist University
Plainview   (806) 296-4706

West Texas A&M University
Canyon   (806) 656-2000

Western Texas College
Snyder   (915) 573-8511

Wiley College
Marshall   (903) 927-2414

UTAH

Hawthorne University
Salt Lake City   (801) 485-1801

Salt Lake Community College
Salt Lake City   (801) 957-4111

Snow College
Ephraim   (801) 283-4021

Southern Utah University
Cedar City   (801) 586-7700

University of Phoenix—Salt Lake City
Salt Lake City   (801) 263-1444

Utah State University
Logan   (801) 797-1000

Utah Valley State College
Orem   (801) 222-8000

Weber State University
Ogden   (801) 626-6000

VERMONT

College of St. Joseph
Rutland   (802) 773-5900

Community Colleges of Vermont
Office of External Programs
Montpelier   (802) 828-4064

Goddard College
Plainfield   (802) 454-8311

Green Mountain College
Poultney   (802) 287-8000

Lyndon State College
Lyndonville   (802) 626-6492

Marlboro College
Marlboro   (802) 257-4333

St. Michael's College
Colchester   (802) 654-2100

School for International Training
Brattleboro   (802) 257-7751

Trinity College
Burlington   (802) 658-0337

Vermont College of Norwich
University
Montpelier   (802) 828-8725

Vermont Technical College
Randolph Center   (802) 728-1243

VIRGINIA

Averett College
Danville   (804) 791-5726

Bluefield College
Bluefield   (540) 326-3682

Bridgewater College
Bridgewater   (540) 828-2501

Central Virginia Community College
Lynchburg   (804) 386-4500

Christopher Newport University
Newport News   (804) 594-7000

Clinch Valley College of the
University of Virginia
Wise   (540) 328-0116

Commonwealth College
Virginia Beach   (804) 499-7900

Eastern Mennonite University
Harrisonburg   (540) 432-4000

George Mason University
Fairfax   (703) 993-1000

Germanna Community College
Locust Grove   (540) 727-3000

Hampden-Sydney College
Hampden-Sydney   (804) 223-6203

Hampton University
Hampton   (804) 727-5324

Hollins College
Hollins College   (540) 362-6223

James Madison University
Harrisonburg   (540) 568-1204

J. Sargeant Reynolds Community
College
Richmond   (804) 371-3029

John Tyler Community College
All Campuses   (804) 796-4000

Liberty University
Lynchburg   (804) 582-2397

Longwood College
Farmville   (804) 395-2048

Mary Baldwin College
Staunton   (800) 822-2460

Mary Washington College
Fredericksburg   (800) 468-5614

Radford University
Radford   (540) 831-5249

Shenandoah University
Winchester   (540) 665-5585

Sweet Briar College
Sweet Briar   (804) 381-6100

Thomas Nelson Community College
Hampton   (804) 825-2800

Union Theological Seminary in
  Virginia
Richmond   (804) 355-0671

University of Richmond
Richmond   (804) 289-8000

University of Virginia
Charlottesville   (804) 924-0311

Virginia Commonwealth University
Richmond   (804) 828-0011

Virginia Intermont College
Bristol   (540) 669-6601

Virginia Military Institute
Lexington   (540) 464-7213

Virginia State University
Petersburg   (804) 524-5901

Washington & Lee University
Lexington   (540) 463-8400

WASHINGTON

Big Bend Community College
Moses Lake   (509) 762-5351

Central Washington University
Ellensburg   (509) 963-3001

City University
Renton   (800) 426-5596

Clover Park Technical College
Lakewood   (206) 589-5800

Eastern Washington University
Cheney   (509) 359-6524

Edmonds Community College
Edmonds   (206) 640-1360

Everett Community College
Everett   (206) 388-9219

Evergreen State College
Olympia   (360) 866-6000

Gonzaga University
Spokane   (509) 328-4220

Green River Community College
Auburn   (206) 833-9111

Henry Cogswell College
Everett   (206) 258-3351

Lutheran Bible Institute of Seattle
Issaquah   (206) 392-0400

Northwest College
Kirkland   (206) 889-7799

Northwest Graduate School of the
  Ministry
Kirkland   (206) 828-7431

Pacific Lutheran University
Tacoma   (206) 535-8870

Puget Sound Christian College
Edmonds   (206) 775-8686

Renton Technical College
Renton   (206) 235-2352

Spokane Community College
Spokane   (509) 533-7006

Spokane Falls Community College
Spokane   (509) 533-3401

Tacoma Community College
Tacoma   (206) 566-5000

Walla Walla College
College Place   (509) 527-2327

Washington State University
Pullman   (509) 335-7878

Western Washington University
Bellingham   (360) 676-3430

Whatcom Community College
Bellingham   (360) 676-2170

Whitman College
Walla Walla   (509) 527-5980

WEST VIRGINIA

Bluefield State College
Bluefield   (304) 327-4000

The College of West Virginia
Beckley   (304) 253-7351

Davis & Elkins College
Elkins   (304) 637-1900

Fairmont State College
Fairmont   (304) 367-4141

Salem-Teikyo University
Salem   (304) 782-5011

Shepherd College
Shepherdstown   (304) 876-5000

University of Charleston
Charleston   (304) 357-4800

West Virginia State College
Institute   (304) 766-3000

West Virginia University at
    Parkersburg
Parkersburg   (304) 424-8000

Wheeling Jesuit University
Wheeling   (800) 873-7665

WISCONSIN

Alverno College
Milwalkee   (414) 382-6072

Bellin College of Nursing
Green Bay   (414) 433-3560

Beloit College
Beloit   (608) 363-2640

Cardinal Stritch College
Milwaukee   (414) 352-5400

Carroll College
Waukesha   (414) 524-7211

Carthage College
Kenosha   (414) 551-6100

Chippewa Valley Technical College
Eau Claire   (715) 833-6200

Concordia University, Wisconsin
Mequon   (414) 243-5700

Edgewood College
Madison   (608) 257-4861

Fox Valley Technical College
Appleton   (414) 735-5600

Gateway Technical College
Racine   (414) 631-7316

Lawrence University
Appleton   (414) 832-6578

Maranatha Baptist Bible College
Watertown   (414) 261-9300

Marian College of Fond Du Lac
Fond Du Lac   (414) 923-7600

Mount Mary College
Milwaukee   (414) 258-4810

Mount Senario College
Ladysmith   (715) 532-5511

Nicolet Area Technical College
Rhinelander   (715) 365-4422

Northland College
Ashland   (715) 682-1699

Ripon College
Ripon   (414) 748-8326

St. Norbert College
De Pere   (414) 337-3781

Silver Lake College
Manitowoc   (414) 684-6691

University of Wisconsin—Stevens
    Point
Stevens Point   (715) 346-0123

University of Wisconsin—River Falls
River Falls   (715) 425-3911

University of Wisconsin—Eau Claire
Eau Claire   (715) 836-3887

University of Wisconsin—La Crosse
La Crosse   (608) 785-8000

University of Wisconsin—Madison
Madison   (608) 262-1234

University of Wisconsin—Parkside
Kenosha   (414) 595-2211

University of Wisconsin—Platteville
Platteville   (608) 342-1321

University of Wisconsin—Stout
Menomonie   (715) 232-1123

University of Wisconsin—Superior
Superior   (715) 394-8218

University of Wisconsin—Whitewater
Whitewater   (414) 472-1234

Viterbo College
La Crosse   (608) 791-0411

Waukesha County Technical College
Pewaukee   (414) 691-5319

Wisconsin Lutheran College
Milwaukee   (414) 443-8800

G L O S S A R Y

NOTE: Many of the words in this glossary have two or more meanings. Here, however, they are defined in only the limited meaning that is particular to their use in discussion of prior learning assessment. For instance, as a verb the word "discipline" can mean chastise, control, correct, punish, train; as a noun it can mean conduct, method, exercise, order, etc. In this glossary it is used only as it refers to an academic area of study.

Adult learner—One who is older than the traditional college student (25+); one who is living away from parents and/or is self-supporting; one whose primary role is other than learner (such as worker, parent, spouse, or retiree).

Articulation—The process by which students can relate what they have already learned to what they want or need to learn. Articulation also can mean relating the learnings for which they are requesting credit to their academic, personal, and professional goals. Articulation is particularly useful in degree program planning.

A somewhat different meaning of articulation refers to agreements among colleges regarding the transfer of credit.

Assessment—The process of defining, documenting, measuring, evaluating, and granting credit for learning acquired through non-college or experientially-gained knowledge, skills, and competencies.

Basic Education—A term usually applied to work in reading, writing, and mathematics designed to bring the student to an eighth- or tenth-grade level in those subjects.

CAEL—Council for Adult and Experiential Learning is an educational association dedicated to the advancement of experiential learning, fostering its valid and reliable assessment, and sponsoring research and publication on its operation and advantages. CAEL is a leader in helping adults take advantage of learning opportunities and get credit for what they know. CAEL does not itself assess individual students' learning nor award academic credit.

Certificate—A document attesting that one has completed a program and gained competency in a specific area (electronics, data processing, etc.). A certificate may entail anything from a single course to a cluster of courses and may or may not carry credit towards a degree.

CEU—Continuing education units are nontraditional education credits, usually awarded for educational experiences that are designed to meet the requirements of professional organizations. For example, teachers, nurses, physicians, and accountants must earn a certain number of CEUs to maintain or enhance their professional status. Some colleges are trying to work out ways to equate CEUs to college credit, but there is as yet no widely accepted standard. Because CEUs have traditionally been measures of time spent in class or workshops rather than measures of learning acquired, CAEL recommends against calibrating CEUs with college credit.

Challenge Exam—An examination given by the instructor of a course to someone who wishes to get credit for the course without having taken it. Typically, the challenge exam is similar or identical to the one that the instructor gives to a class at the end of the semester.

CLEP—The College Level Examination Program is a standardized examination program offering students the opportunity to earn college credit in many common academic areas. (See appendix E.)

Concentration—(See "Major.")

Continuing Education—Courses offered on a credit or not-for-credit basis that specifically target adults, usually part-time. These courses may be offered by colleges and universities or by high schools, churches, YMCA/YWCAs, community adult education programs, etc.

Correspondence program (or course)—A structured college syllabus or set of lessons presented in print form that offers the student an opportunity to work independently at home, reading, doing assignments, and taking tests. Usually student and instructor keep in touch by mail, but some programs are using telephones and computers extensively. Some of the colleges found in appendix D may offer correspondence courses.

Credit—The common measure of progress toward graduation in most U.S. colleges and universities. Usually one (1) credit is granted for each class hour per week in a 14 to 16 week semester. Courses may be worth anywhere from one to five credits, with three (3) credits the most common. Though the numbers vary slightly from school to school, the requirement for most associates degrees is a total of 60 credits; for bachelors degrees, 120 credits.

Curriculum—A prescribed set of courses for an area of specialization (e.g., engineering, biology, political science).

DANTES—Dantes Subject Standardized Tests (DSSTs) are standardized credit-by-examination tests offering students the opportunity to earn college credit in many common academic and technical areas. (See appendix E.)

Degrees—College degrees are earned by completing a specified number of courses or other studies in accordance with a program design acceptable to the college or university and subject to their requirements. The common degrees are:

Associate of arts (AA), associate of science (AS) or associate of applied science (AAS)—two year degrees, usually granted by community colleges.

Bachelor of arts (BA), bachelor of science (BS) or bachelor of fine arts (BFA) or bachelor of professional studies (BPS)—four year degrees, granted by colleges and universities.

Master of arts (M.A.) or master of science (M.S.)—graduate degrees, granted by universities, usually involve taking at least one full year beyond the bachelor's degree plus writing a thesis.

Doctor of philosophy (Ph.D.)—graduate degree, granted by universities. Some people take a master's degree first. Others go right on to the Ph.D., which will then take somewhat longer. The Ph.D. course work is usually followed by a major piece of research, called a dissertation.

Discipline—A broad field of study, such as history, psychology, or computer science (as opposed to "subject," which is more specialized, such as "history of the post-reconstruction period" or "adolescent psychology").

Distance learning—An expanded version of correspondence learning, distance learning offers another way for students who cannot attend classes regularly to learn though independent study, television, computers, e-mail, video hookups to classes, etc. Schools with distance learning programs (see appendix D) appeal to adults who have the ability to work well on their own. Contact with the instructor may be maintained through correspondence, fax, phones, computers, e-mail or other electronic means.

Documentation—Evidence that supports the claim for credit for prior learning experience. Documentation may be in the form of transcripts, professional licenses or certificates, records of apprenticeships, certificates of completion of company or union training, official job descriptions, letters, news clippings, products produced by the student such as books, paintings, computer programs, hand-crafted objects, etc.

Electives—Courses taken as part of one's degree program that are not required for the major, but that are chosen from the school's offerings after all requirements for the major, general education, or other school stipulations have been met. Well-chosen electives can round out a program, give it breadth, and enable students to sample subjects in the humanities, and social and physical sciences that can enrich their lives.

Evaluation—The process by which one or more faculty persons determine the credit equivalency of a specific unit of learning.

Evidence—(See "Documentation.")

Experiential learning—Any learning in which the learner is in direct touch with the realities being studied. This learning may be sponsored (as in work/study arrangements, internships, apprentice-ships) or it may be acquired informally through hands-on experi-ence and practice through work, travel, personal development, or community service.

External degree program—An academic degree program that en-ables students to complete their studies without necessarily attend-ing class. Sometimes called "colleges without walls," external de-gree programs are especially designed for the adult part-time learner who needs flexibility and who can work independently. (See "correspondence program" and "distance learning.")

Faculty—Those who are responsible for teaching in colleges and universities. The common titles given to faculty, in ascending order, are: lecturer, instructor, assistant professor, associate professor, pro-fessor. In addition, schools may employ teaching assistants who are graduate students and part-time or adjunct faculty who have ex-pertise in a specific area. A few colleges call their faculty "mentors" or "learning facilitators," regardless of their rank.

Full-time student—One who is registered for 12 semester hours or more for credit.

GED (General Education Development)—The equivalent of a high school degree, the GED is earned through a standardized national examination, which measures educational development in five areas. This exam is designed for persons who have not completed the formal requirements for a high school diploma. A great many high schools and adult basic learning schools sponsor courses designed to help the adult prepare for the GED exam. In 1995, over 523,000 people earned GED credentials.

Learning component—A single, identifiable chunk of learning that is part of a larger "subject." Thus, Pascal computer language is a learning component of computer science; knowledge of OSHA procedures is a learning component of personnel management; understanding why infants exhibit grasping behavior is a learning component of child development.

Major—The subject or discipline in which a student specializes. Using it as a noun, one can have a major in math, sociology, business studies, etc. As a verb, one can major in these subjects. Each school has regulations that determine how many courses must be completed in one's major subject to fulfill the requirements of the degree.

Measurement—Ascertaining the nature of the specific learning acquired by a person—its quality, quantity, and level. In most schools, measurement of learning for the purpose of prior learning assessment is done by a faculty member in the appropriate discipline or area.

Minor—In some colleges, students are required to develop a secondary area of concentration in addition to their major (see above). For example, a political science major may have a minor in Russian language.

Part-time student—One who is registered for less than 12 hours of credit per semester.

PONSI (Program on Non-Collegiate Sponsored Instruction)—Conducted by the American Council on Education, this program evaluates courses sponsored by corporations, unions, and the armed services, and issues program guides which recommend credit for those deemed equivalent to college courses.

Portfolio—A document compiled by the learner in support of his or her request for credit. Although requirements may vary somewhat from school to school, typically, the portfolio consists of the following sections:

Essay—narrative that describes the learner's background and career and education goals, explains how the prior learnings were acquired, and discusses how these learnings fit into his or her proposed degree program and overall education and career plans.

Identification—description of the learnings for which the student is requesting credit, including a definition of the learning in curriculum or competency-based terms.

Articulation—explanation of how these learnings were acquired, relating them to the student's overall education and career objectives and, in some cases, to the proposed degree program.

Documentation—evidence that the learnings are valid as described.

Request for credit—list of the specific learnings for which credit is sought, with numerical equivalents.

Postsecondary education—Education occurring after high school. This may include credit and non-credit courses.

Practicum—A "hands-on" experience of applying classroom learning to a real life situation. Thus, a major in child psychology may include a practicum spent working in a child-care center.

Prerequisites—Those courses that must be completed before taking something else. Thus, beginning and intermediate Spanish may be prerequisites for Spanish literature; introduction to chemistry may be a prerequisite for nuclear chemistry.

Registrar—The college official responsible for keeping records on the enrollment and academic standing of students. The registrar also must attest to the validity of transcripts submitted for admission to advanced standing.

Resume—Although usually defined as a summary of one's work experience, for purposes of assessment, the resume includes all experiences that may have resulted in learning: dates, sources, the nature of the work (or hobby or independent learning of any kind), the learnings acquired.

Semester—A period of time (usually 14 to 18 weeks) into which colleges divide the school year. Most courses last one semester and may be scheduled from two to five hours each week of that semester. There are usually two semesters in a college year, plus, in many institutions, a summer semester. Some schools have developed a *trimester* or *quarter* system which may change both the period of time and the number of class hours (or credits) per week.

Semester hour—This is usually defined as 15 hours of class time over the course of the semester, or one hour per week. Thus, a three hour course will meet three hours per week for 15 weeks for three credits. (Most schools assume that the student also spends two hours of preparation for every hour spent in the classroom.)

Syllabus—An outline of the main points to be covered in a course. A syllabus may also include the requirements of the course or the competencies expected to be acquired, as well as a list of the required textbook(s) and assignments.

Transcript—An official school document that lists the courses taken by a student, grades and credit earned, and degree awarded. The imprint of the school seal and authorized signature on the transcript attest to its validity.

I N D E X

A

action plan, xviii, 38–41
adult learners, xiii–xiv, xvii–xix, 64–65, 219
  advantages, 3, 153
  defined, 219
  numbers on campus, 1–3
  profiled adult learners, 11–21 (see also Anna, Dorene, Joan, Max, Scott)
  presence on campus, 1–4
  welcomed by colleges, 5–6
adult learning, importance of, xiii–xiv
adult student services, 5–6, 153
advanced placement, 76, 171
American Council on Education (ACE), 78, 83, 175–76 (see also PONSI)
Anna, 19–20, 35, 81–82, 96, 98–99, 120–21, 145

articulation, 74, 219–20
assessment, 71–82, 83–130, *passim* (see also prior learning assessment)
  defined, 220
  what you need to find out about it, 57–59
autobiography, 102 (see also essay)

B

basic education, 220
basic skills, 9–10, 153–55

C

CAEL, xv, xix, 59, 67–8, 159, 191, 220
campus
  catalog information on, 55–57
  touring the, 59, 132–34
career planning, xiv, 23–41

action plan, 38–41
connections between career
  planning and PLA, 25–26
defining career goals, 26–28
importance of, 23–26
reading social trends, 37–38
resources and materials, xiv, 24, 36–
  38, 161–62
Carnegie formula, 123
certificate, 53, 220
certificate programs, 52
college admission, when to apply for,
  10
college catalogs, 55–57, 122
college level learning, 98–100, 128,
  159
college terminology, 51–52, 219–26
college transcripts (see transcripts)
colleges, 3–4, 5–6, 46–48 (also see
  schools)
  articulation agreements among, 74
  choosing the right one, 43–61
  follow-up activities, 59
  important questions to ask about,
    55–57
colleges and universities with
  comprehensive PLA programs, xiv,
  xv, 191–218
consumer of education, smart, xviii,
  43–61
continuing education, 221
cost of school, 147
credit, 51–52, 58, 71–74, 221
  by certification, 72
  by examination, 71, 74–77, 171–74
  Carnegie formula, 123
  CEU (continuing education unit),
    52, 220
  determining your credit request,
    116–23
    college course method, 116–21
    learning components method,
      121–22
    using a college catalog, 122

for completion of evaluated
  programs, 72, 78–9, 175–76
for professional licenses or
  certificates, 72, 79, 174–75
transcripts, 72–73
versus non-credit, 53
curriculum, 222

D

defining your learning, 65–67, 85–98
  (see also identification of learning)
degrees, 52–53, 222
discipline, 222
distance learning, 48–51, 167–69, 222
documentation of learning, 85, 103–
  16, 222–23
  avoiding overkill, 115–16
  direct and indirect, 104–05
  letters of, 111–15
  letters requesting, 108–10
  purpose of, 103
  resources, 104–05, 106
  steps to obtaining, 105–07
  worksheet, 185–86
Dorene, 15–17, 26–27, 81, 93, 98–99,
  108–10, 113–15, 120, 126–27, 148

E

editing, 103, 128
electives, 223
essay, 85, 101–03, 126
evaluated programs, credit for, 71,
  77–78, 175
evaluation, 71–82 passim, 115, 129–30,
  223
evidence (see documentation)
examinations, credit by, 74–7, 171–74
  ACT-PEP Regents College Exams,
    57, 75, 77, 83, 172
  Advanced Placement Program
    (APP), 76, 171
  challenge exam, 76, 221

CLEP, 57, 74–75, 77, 81, 83, 172–73, 221, 245
DANTES Subject Standardized Tests, 57, 75, 79, 83, 173, 221, 246
Graduate Record Exam (GRE), 76
Job Ready Level Assessment, 76, 173–74
oral (see also faculty evaluation), 76
professional certifying exam, 77
written exam, 74–76
exercises
1-1 Then and Now, 5
3-1 Why Do You Want to Go Back to School, 26–27
3-2 Assessing Your Values, 29–32
3-3 Your Skills, 36
3-4 Developing Your Own Action Plan, 38–40
4-1 Musts and Wants, 45–46
4-2 Important Questions to Ask About Colleges, 55–57
4-3 What You Need to Find Out About Assessment, 57–59
5-1 Focusing on a Learning Experience, 65
8-1 Pie Chart System of Time Management, 137
8-2 Prioritizing Tasks, 139
8-3 Surveying Your Support System, 141–42
experiential learning, xiv, 6–9, 68 f.n., 223
four-stage cycle of, 8
external degree program, 167–69, 223 (see also distance learning, independent learning)
extracurricular activities, importance of, 157

F
faculty evaluation, 115, 118, 129–30
financial aid, 145–47
full-time student, 223

G
GED (General Education Development), 66, 224
getting the information you need, 53–55
going back to school, xviii

H
hedging your bets, 60

I
identification of learning, 85, 86–100
guidelines for, 100–02
independent learning, xiv, 48–51, 167–69

J
Joan, 15, 48, 79, 92, 94–95, 98–100, 118, 148

L
learner, the reader as, xvii–xviii
learning, 64–67
abilities of adults, 3–4
acquired outside the classroom, 83–84
broadening of learnings presented for assessment, xiv
component, 224
extra-collegiate, 83–84
focusing on a learning experience, 65–67
getting credit for _____, xviii
_____ assessment worksheet, 181–84
_____ components, 101 f.n.
_____ vs. experience, 84
respect for, xviii
sources of, 66
value of, x, 67
why we learn, 66

learning styles, 7–9, 66
libraries, 37, 55, 133–34, 154–55
licenses and certificates, 72, 79, 174–75
lifelong learning, 6

M

major, 224
Max, 17–19, 81, 93–96, 98–100, 110–13, 144–45, 148
minor, 224
money matters, 145–47

N

narrative (see essay)
non-collegiate sponsored instruction, 57 (see also PONSI)

O

older adult learning, xiv
on-the-job learning, xiv

P

part-time student, 224
performance evaluation, 115
planning, life and career, 23–42
    defining career goals, 25–28
    developing your action plan, 38–41
    importance of, 23–25
    resources for, 36–38
    values assessment, 29–31
    why plan?, 23–25
PONSI (Guide for the Program on Non-Collegiate Sponsored Instruction, ACE), 78, 81, 83, 123, 175–76, 224–25
portfolio
    basic components of, 125–27
    cover page, 125
    definition, 84, 225
    duplicate copy, 128
    essay or narrative, 126
    identification of prior learning, 85–88

learning components and their documentation, 126–27
    neatness counts, 128
    organizing, 123–27
    parts of, 85
    revising, 128
    submitting the, 128
    table of contents, 126
portfolio-assisted assessment, xiv, 57–59, 72, 83–130 (see also portfolio)
postsecondary education, 225
practicum, 225
prerequisites, 225
prior learning assessment (PLA), xiii, 6, 56, 57–59, 63–70, 72
    colleges and universities with comprehensive programs, 191–218
    defined, 63, 67–68
    history of, 67–68
    methods used, 71–82
    questions to ask, 57–59
    standards of good practice, xix, 59, 68, 159–60
    through testing, 57, 74–77
    value of, 20, 68–70

Q

quality assurance (PLA), xix, 59, 61, 68, 159–60

R

reading effectively, 154 (see also basic skills)
registrar, 225
resumé, 226

S

schools (see also colleges and universities)
    campus tour, 59
    catalogs, 55–57, 122
    choosing the right one, 43–46, 54–59

finding information about, 53–59
kinds of, 46–48
terminology, 46–48 (also see
Glossary)
Scott, 13, 34–35, 79, 80, 81, 88–89, 90–
91, 100, 119–20
semester, 226
skills
assessment, 32–35
categories, 33
lists, 34–35, 163–65
transferable, 36
"speaking college," 46–48, 51–53
student services, 134, 153–54
study habits, 148–55
creating a study plan, 150–51
finding the right place to study,
148–50
study skills, 151–55
study tips, 44, 187–89
support system, 141–45
defined, 141
surveying its strengths and
weaknesses, 141–42
negotiating a family contract, 144–
45
syllabus, 226

T

taking notes, 154
testing and assessment, xv
testing programs, 171–74
test-taking, 77
time management, 135–41
classic system, 138–40
energy cycles, 140
pie chart system, 137–38
time vampires, 140
transcript, 72–73, 130, 226
transition back to school, 18
trouble shooting, 155

V

values assessment, 28–32